D0881134

SALZBURG

Salzburg

City of Culture

Hubert Nowak

Translated by Peter Lewis

First published in Great Britain in 2020 by
The Armchair Traveller
4 Cinnamon Row
London SW11 3TW

Original title: *Lesereise Salzburg. Die kleine Stadt als Weltbühne.*
Originally published in Austria by: Picus Verlag Ges.m.b.H., Vienna
© 2016 Picus Verlag Ges.m.b.H., Vienna

English translation copyright © 2020 Peter Lewis

Hbk ISBN: 978-1-909961-68-5
Pbk ISBN: 978-1-909961-71-5
eISBN: 978-1-909961-69-2

Typeset in Garamond by MacGuru Ltd
Printed in the UK by Clays Ltd, Elcograf S.p.A.

www.hauspublishing.com
@hauspublishing

Contents

1

Love Takes Time

And it's not always as deep as it is with Mozart

I T WASN'T A CASE of love at first sight. Nor even at second. And yet, the way things are now, you'd think the French kiss was never going to end. It might be a valid criticism of the modern lover that she took her time realising that she was in love. But the fact that she does love is beyond question.

Love takes time. Sometimes it only blossoms after fifty-one years. At least, that's how it was with Salzburg. When Joannes Chrysostomus Wolfgangus Theophilus Mozart, the wonder of his age, came calling in the hope of finding fertile ground in which to strike roots and transcend the role he had been assigned up until then – some kind of freak show – he was shown the door. In all likelihood, by then the corpulent aristocrats' and cassock-wearers' appetite for the extraordinary was already jaded. The fact that he was quite extraordinary was beyond doubt, but was there anything more to him? Perhaps his father was a prototype of those pushy ice-dancer mothers you find nowadays, whose firm conviction that their children are uniquely gifted only gets people's backs up rather than helps. In any event, he was given the cold shoulder.

The shoulder in question belonged to Prince-Archbishop Colloredo, who was of the opinion that it would be sufficient merely to appoint Mozart as the court organist. The eccentric young man's aptitudes were clearly too eccentric. At the tender age of twenty-five, and as yet unmarried, he was self-confident and hungry enough to seek his fortune elsewhere and so simply packed his bags and quit Salzburg for Vienna, where his future wife Constanze was already living. There he carved out a career for himself and was fêted. Ten years later, though, he was dead – still a controversial figure, but by now world famous. And yet he was buried in a pauper's grave and quickly faded into obscurity. His fame back then was like that of a circus performer today: people admired and marvelled at him, but they did not keep him in their hearts. Once dead, he was forgotten.

Yet fifty-one years after his death, a monument to him was erected in his native city. The first of many.

Nowadays, you stumble upon reminders of this *genius loci* at every twist and turn in the Old Town quarter of Salzburg: Mozartplatz, the Mozarteum, Mozart's birthplace in the Getreidegasse, the house where Mozart lived on Makartplatz, the House for Mozart in the festival district, Café Mozart, and the Mozart memorial on Ursulinenplatz. Musicians now joke that to enter Salzburg you need a 'Mozart-ball-proof vest' (*Mozartkugelsichere Weste* – a pun on the confection Mozartkugeln, balls of marzipan and nougat coated in chocolate, and *kugelsicher*, 'bullet-proof').

Yet for all this, his true genius is preserved in thousands of hastily jotted-down musical notes and in a series of witty and rather crude letters, as well as being acknowledged in hundreds of scholarly studies. In other words, Mozart is alive and well, or at least the cult surrounding him is.

It was only several decades after his death that the idea was mooted of putting him on a pedestal in Salzburg. A society was founded, though in those days it was called a 'committee'. Even so, the city's liberal bourgeoisie had a lot of convincing to do, with the city fathers and the Church still opposed to the idea, before finally the square that was then called Michaelerplatz was chosen as a site for the monument. The 3-metre-high statue, designed by Ludwig von Schwanthaler and cast in Munich, was made of bronze and was hollow. In those days, no one had even dreamt of things like the EU internal market and open borders, so of course it was only natural that someone should use the empty void to smuggle tobacco. How typical of Mozart, one might say. Yet another scandal. But from that point on, there was no holding back the city's outpouring of love for its native son.

Other deserving people with Salzburg connections have not had nearly so much in the way of fulsome recognition bestowed upon them.

For instance, a certain Philippus Theophrastus Aureolus Bombastus von Hohenheim, better known as Paracelsus, died in 1541 in Salzburg. In actual fact, this restless figure only lived properly in the city on two occasions, and even those sojourns were quite brief; Salzburg was just one of the many places he stopped on his journeys between Switzerland and Carinthia. His gravestone at St Sebastian's cemetery was only erected 200 years after his death. Even so, this polymath, who was a physician, alchemist, philosopher and astrologer, gave his name to the first-ever private medical university in Austria, which was founded in Salzburg in 2002. And one of the sites where hands-on medical teaching is conducted in the city is at the Christian Doppler Clinic in the suburb of Lehen.

The name of this psychiatric clinic, which was formerly designated as a lunatic asylum, derives from someone who was actually born and bred in Salzburg. The mathematician and physicist Christian Doppler was born in 1803 on the Makartplatz, where a commemorative plaque was unveiled in his honour a hundred years later. A research laboratory and a grammar school on the banks of the Salzach both also bear his name (after all, almost everyone has at least heard of the acoustic effect that is named after him), as well as a crater on the moon. But that's a long way away. One peculiarity even links Doppler to Mozart: the precise site of Doppler's grave – in the San Michele cemetery in Venice – has never been pinpointed either.

As a general rule, when commemorating its famous sons and daughters, Salzburg (like Austria as a whole, in fact) makes little distinction as to whether they were born or died there. Or even just spent a brief sojourn there. Take Alexander von Humboldt, for instance. This great man, another polymath, was a Berliner through and through. As a natural scientist, he travelled throughout almost the entire world, including Salzburg of course. Constantinople was one place he didn't visit, though in 1804 he is supposed to have exclaimed: 'I think that Salzburg, Naples and Constantinople are the most beautiful places on Earth.' This, plus a stay of several months' duration at number 14 Schanzlgasse, was enough for Salzburg to put up a plaque and to name a street, a student hall of residence, a restaurant, and a viewing platform on the Mönchsberg (much frequented by suicides) after him.

The city's beauty also captivated many others throughout the ages. It is said of the writer Peter Handke, who spent almost a decade living on the Richterhöhe, right on the summit of the Mönchsberg, that he was once beaten up by a group of rowdy tourists whom he'd just exhorted, in vain, to conduct themselves with a bit of decorum in such a venerable city as Salzburg.

Admittedly, this lack of decorum doesn't always manifest itself as rowdiness. Sometimes it takes the form of a vehement written denunciation of the fact that the commercialised symbiosis between a composer and his birthplace obscures every other connection. That has a longer-lasting impact, as someone who is abused in writing finds it difficult to ever show love again. The playwright Thomas Bernhard was well aware of that, but simply accepted that the city he criticised so roundly, indeed insulted, doesn't really like him, even now.

This despite the fact that his plays are staged there. At best, Salzburgers hold their noses when invoking his name, as if to affirm that he really was in the wrong. With merciless cruelty, Bernhard poked his finger into the open wound of profiteering and superficiality. At points, his autobiography reads like a final reckoning: 'Everything in this city runs counter to creativity. And even though it maintains ever more frequently and vehemently that the opposite is the case, there's a fundamental hypocrisy about this, and its greatest passion is banality, and wherever imagination does rear its head, it is quickly eradicated.'

When he was still a young journalist with the local newspaper, the *Demokratischer Volksblatt*, alongside court reports Bernhard penned paeans of praise to the peace-loving people of the region and their rich cultural heritage, as well as to the countryside and the beauty of the city. His fellow dramatist Carl Zuckmayer, who spent some time before the war living as if 'in paradise' near Salzburg, had put forward Bernhard's name to the newspaper, which was an organ of the Austrian Socialist Party, in 1952.

At some point, Bernhard underwent a Damascene conversion. But because he was wont to dissect everything about Austria that irked him with a razor-scarp scalpel, people like to relativise his attack on Salzburg. Oh well, they say, Bernhard was a thoroughly grouchy individual at the best of times, and he laid into everyone and everything. Because of what he saw as its narrow-minded, petty-bourgeois mentality, he once called the city a 'Death Museum'. The thing that most infuriated him was its half-hearted dissociation from the remnants of Nazism and its consciously lackadaisical reappraisal of this period in the country's history. And there's no denying that Salzburg laid itself open to such an attack.

It would have been fully consistent with his stance on this issue if Bernhard had also laid into one of his literary 'fore-bears' in the city, namely Hermann Bahr, and his Teutonic jingoism. This writer, who was born in Linz in 1863, spent four years in Salzburg as a young man. In an autobiographical sketch, he later wrote:

> I arrived in Salzburg at the age of fourteen. My grandmother was born there, and my great-grandfather had been a master gunsmith at Salzburg Fortress. I was completely overwhelmed at the sight of the city. Here a solid, German character of the Bavarian type is imbued with a sunny southern radiance, and when the wind blows in from the High Tauern [a mountain range in the Central Alps] you can sense the presence of the lovely land of Italy, and there's a breath of it on all the roofs and towers of the city; all the things that go to make up the German 'yearning for the South' can be found here.

Stefan Zweig once characterised Hermann Bahr as an 'intellectual brawler who swings his fists about wildly in support of all the things he senses are up and coming.' Zweig no doubt coined that memorable phrase for Bahr thanks to his championing of the new artistic movements of the period – Impressionism in painting, the trend towards simplicity and lack of ornamentation in architecture, and the philosophy of Nietzsche. Paying homage to the 'German character' was then considered good manners; only later did it prove to be disastrous.

Unlike with Thomas Bernhard, commemorating Stefan Zweig in Salzburg doesn't put anyone's nose out of joint. Starting from the Linzergasse and crossing the Imbergstiege, a steep road leads up to the Paschinger Schlössl, in the vicinity of the Capuchin Monastery. To number 5 Kapuzinerberg, to be precise. The monument to Zweig is just a little way up the road from there. Even further up, you'll find yet another Mozart memorial, marking the place where he composed *The Magic Flute*. So even there, Mozart is placed above Zweig. Born in Vienna, Zweig purchased the former hunting lodge of Archbishop Paris Graf von Lodron in 1917 and lived there until 1934.

Zweig was a seasoned traveller who visited many countries, from America to Russia, whenever he didn't happen to have notable guests staying. Maurice Ravel is said to have visited him on the Kapuzinerberg, as did Thomas Mann and James Joyce. But before long Zweig, characterising his itinerant existence, was noting: 'My empty suitcases are yawning at me. I urgently need to stuff their gaping maws.' He only described Salzburg shortly before he left to go into exile in England. In 1933, as if in pastel shades, he painted a picture of the city for those who were unfamiliar with it. The Romans, the archbishops, the mountains, the climate, the salt – for Zweig, these were all constituent elements of the city's aura, which had been made stone: 'Like few other cities, Salzburg knows how to resoundingly resolve into stone and atmosphere things that would otherwise in reality be in stark contradiction to one another. What's more, it learnt this secret, this resolution of dissonances into harmony, from music.'

A far less compelling force than that acting on Stefan Zweig drew the poet Georg Trakl away from Salzburg. Neither Vienna nor Innsbruck could contain this melancholic genius and, in contrast to the pastel-hued Zweig and especially the gaudily coloured Mozart, his path through life seems gloomy and Stygian. To this day no one really knows whether his early death from a drug overdose was an accident or suicide. He too was a critic of the city. Unsurprisingly, it's not that aspect of Trakl but rather his impressive body of lyrical work that the city and the province of Salzburg both recognise with the award of the Georg Trakl Prize for Poetry every ten years, on the anniversary of his birth and his death respectively. And every day, if you should so choose, you can read a poem of his carved on a stone plaque at the site of the Zum Weißen Engel chemist's shop where he once worked as a pharmacist. 'By the bare wall, the lonely one wanders with his stars,' runs one of its stanzas. The house on the Waagplatz where he was born, though, is anything but bare, with its bustling art gallery and workshop. In tune with the self-image Salzburg is keen to promote, there's a crossover between genres going on here.

Yet the greatest crossover between genres that occurs in this city is undoubtedly when the talk turns from Mozart to a certain Richard Rodgers. The man in question was an American, who had little to do with Salzburg but who laid the foundations for what is at least the second most important tourist attraction in the city: the cult surrounding *The Sound of Music*.

This musical, about the novice Maria who wins the hearts of the widower Baron von Trapp and his seven children, captivated theatre-goers on Broadway in their hundreds of thousands. When the story of this family choir, who made a successful career out of performing folk music first in Salzburg and then in exile in the USA, was filmed, the picturesque images of Salzburg were beamed around the world, time and time again. Only Salzburg kept its distance from the musical and the film. Quite why it did so is a real puzzle. Maybe a fear of anything that touched on the Nazi period was one reason, or perhaps it was an unacknowledged envy that Americans, of all people, should have been the ones to make a movie about Austrian folk culture that was substantially better than any of the home-grown offerings produced up until then. Whatever the case, this most successful location placement in the history of film was decried as being kitsch, and the name of the von Trapp family crosses people's lips as often as that of Thomas Bernhard – namely, almost never. And if they are ever mentioned, it's with disdain (which in both cases is quite unfair). In 2015, a new film was made about the von Trapp family, from the point of view of the eldest sister, Agathe. Once again it used the prettiest locations in the city but steered clear of the clichés of the American musical film. Instead, it was 'closer to reality' and pulled no punches about cruel blows of fate, conflicts between the children and their stepmother, and politics. It wasn't a smash hit.

The fact is that the musical film of 1965 was one of the highest-grossing movies in cinema history, and it is still being screened repeatedly on television in many countries (except in Austria). As a result it draws hundreds of thousands of visitors to see the original places where it was shot. So, you can follow in the footsteps of Julie Andrews and go round the various locations by bus, bike, horse-drawn cab or even rickshaw. Or take a bus tour starting at the Mirabellplatz and taking in Leopoldskron Palace, the summer house at Hellbrunn, the convent at Nonnberg where Maria and the Baron actually got married, and the church in Mondsee that was used for the wedding scene in the film. And if you also fancy breakfasting in Leopoldskron Palace like the von Trapps did, visiting the house where they lived, gazing in awe at the mountain redoubt of Hohenwerfen, and humming along to 'Do-Re-Mi' on the upland meadow in the Salzkammergut where Maria taught the children that song, then you'd better allow for a full nine hours on a bus.

There's only one place you can't visit on these tours: the Sound of Music Museum. That's because it doesn't exist: where and how to establish one has been the subject of decades of political wrangling. It's supposedly due to be built sometime in the Mirabellgarten. In the meantime, a small, privately run exhibition in the Getreidegasse at least serves to fill the gap for von Trapp-addicted tourists from around the world.

Fair enough; it also took some time before Mozart was given his due. Even so, we're already past the fifty-one-year mark.

2

Mozart Would be a Jazzman Nowadays

Or he would have written The Sound of Music

WELL, WELL ... *The Sound of Music*, eh? Surely, I thought, in this city, you'd be hard put to find anyone who'd touch these songs with a bargepole.

How wrong can you be?

'This music is just crazy! I only got to know *The Sound of Music* late on, because it has such a clichéd reputation that I shunned it for years. I only went to see the film when I had a family of my own and took my four kids along, and I was blown away by Julie Andrews and all the fantastic compositions. "My Favourite Things" is just such a beautiful song, I found myself thinking, wow, if only I could have written something like that! We listen to it non-stop now.' The man sitting in Café Bazar pauses in his breathless monologue just long enough to take a sip of his tea. 'In its genre, this music's in a class of its own. Mozart and *The Sound of Music* – they're both mass-market products of real quality. There's no comparing them, of course, but each of them is totally unique and has broad appeal.' And this man knows a thing or two about Mozart. To be sure, as a fan of 'Maria', 'Do-Re-Mi' and 'Edelweiss', he's something of a Johnny-come-lately. But as a musician, he's anything but. My interlocutor is Benjamin Schmid, the world-renowned violinist. Aged fifteen, he won a place at the Mozarteum, and now he's a professor there. He can bring tears to your eyes with his renditions of sunbeams and raindrops from Vivaldi's *Four Seasons*. He knows every concert hall from Toronto to Tokyo and has filled them all with his performances of the works of Korngold and Mozart. And without a moment's hesitation, he declares: '*The Sound of Music*'s probably far better known than Mozart; wherever you go in the world, people recognise it.'

His opinion soon finds corroboration. Another giant of the international music scene likes to hang out and drink the odd cappuccino at the café in Hangar 7, the solitary example of modernist architecture in Salzburg and a temple to *haute cuisine*. Sabina Hank, a jazz pianist, singer, composer and arranger of world renown, has a young daughter. In order to be able to pursue her career, Sabina has already engaged the services of three au pairs, all from the Philippines. They were all well educated, and yet 'Not one of them knew who Mozart was. Unbelievable! The last of them even wondered why the name kept cropping up all over the city: "Who is this guy?" she asked me. So then I played her a couple of pieces, "Eine kleine Nachtmusik" for instance. She knew the melody but not the title.' But when the au pairs arrived, their eyes shone as they rhapsodised about how thrilled they were to be in the city of *The Sound of Music*.

Shortly thereafter, Sabina Hank was due to give a concert in China. A journalist there asked her what numbers from *The Sound of Music* she was going to play. She hadn't actually planned to play any, and in fact only knew 'My Favourite Things', so she set about writing an arrangement for it that very same night in her hotel room. It proved to be a resounding success. What's more: 'It blew my mind!' Back in Salzburg, she immediately sought out a record store and bought the CD of the soundtrack and a DVD of the film. 'I was so moved by it I cried. I suddenly realised why it was such a global phenomenon. It was a revelation to me, I was gobsmacked, I sat down at my grand piano and knew I simply had to start rearranging the whole thing.'

She struck a deal for world rights with the normally very unforthcoming music publishers and set to work on her own, new version of *The Sound of Music*. She completely rearranged and reinterpreted 'this brilliant music' and added one brand new section of her own composition. Inevitably, there will be a world tour to premiere it, starting in Salzburg in 2021.

When negotiating her deal with the record company, she said, the fact that she was from Salzburg had clearly been an advantage. 'It's a distinct plus point in the music industry.' Benjamin Schmid also confirms that. Austrian musicians are especially welcome at a Mozart festival that is held regularly in Colombia. 'Close on a hundred concerts in Bogotá in three days, exclusively Mozart, so it's only natural we should cash in on that. Not to mention Japan.' Mozart is like some universal 'Open Sesame'. 'Quite simply, he was the ultimate musical talent. There's a natural order in his music that the rest of us can only dream of achieving in our lives. He just didn't put a foot wrong, and everything has its proper place. It's like it all just flowed automatically from his fingertips,' gushes Schmid. Mozart's music is understood in all cultures, 'and it clearly suits all levels of musical awareness.'

According to the Austrian composer Friedrich Gulda, Mozart was a 'great benefactor' because his music conveys such an incredibly positive mood. Yet by way of setting his musical hierarchy in proper context, Schmid concedes that Mozart was by no means the supreme patriarch – that was Johann Sebastian Bach – while 'the most significant figure for us musicians was undoubtedly Beethoven.' But little Wolfie was just the most brilliant of them all, a free spirit and a true musical revolutionary of his age, who even as a child was put on a pedestal and hailed as a genius.

Sabina Hank was also a 'child prodigy', though she never saw herself in that light. 'I didn't want to hear that label, because the expectations start to weigh you down and the pressure just grows and grows.' When she was three or four, her parents discovered that she had perfect pitch. At the age of five, the synaesthetic Sabina entered the Mozarteum, one of the youngest pupils ever to be admitted. She experiences sounds as colours. To her, Stravinsky's *The Rite of Spring* is a riot of colour. 'At the entrance exam, the timpani were bigger than me.' And at that tender age, she already found herself thrust into the unforgiving system of competition and achievement that is the world of music.

Even then, Mozart was far and away her favourite composer. His 'Ave verum corpus' can still make her melt nowadays. But having to practise his sonatas, or worse still Bach's *Inventions*, drove her at the age of twelve to seek some release elsewhere. The catalyst was a disc by Charlie Parker. 'I had no idea at that stage that this was jazz, I just knew it was where I wanted to go.' Away from Bach and Mozart, ideally still performing only composers like Gershwin and Debussy from the classical canon, and towards 'Parker's Mood'. She managed to win over her teachers, who were impressed by her enthusiasm.

Sabina Hank reckons that her musical path would surely have been a different one if she hadn't been from Salzburg 'because the environment you grow up in leaves a really strong impression on you. And Salzburg is a global brand.' But her inner penchant for jazz, for freedom of musical expression, was independent of location, she claims. Of course, she concedes, she'd been influenced by Mozart, by his liveliness, his approach to music as a language, and as a form of improvisation. That was like jazz. 'Mozart was a really great improviser, as was Bach.'

The 1980s Austrian singer-songwriter Falco ('Rock Me, Amadeus') famously cast Mozart in the role of a pop star. And, Hank maintains, 'I feel sure that Mozart would be a jazzman nowadays, and a very popular one at that.' She didn't doubt it for an instant. 'After all, once he'd written something down, that wasn't the end of it, he was constantly on the move and his music was always in the moment. Improvisation is nothing more than ongoing composition from one moment to the next. The brilliant thing about Mozart was how everything he composed was just so perfect. Every note is right. There's nothing there that you would change. The sheer vitality of it! Charlie Parker's got that too. Parker's really pretty close to Mozart.'

Benjamin Schmid is too. Certainly when he's playing Mozart, but also as a jazz musician. He also sees Mozart as being close to jazz. 'There's no doubt that he reinvented his music every time he played it.'

Few musicians have been so comprehensively dissected by scholars as Mozart. All the biographical details have been picked clean, so contemporary research into Mozart tends to focus heavily on interpretation. Relying on knowledge of historical authenticity, the name of the game is to make the musical experience in a concert as exciting as possible. However, this can sometimes be taken too far. 'This fiddling about, say over whether the trill should be played from the top at this point or not, or over whether it should be repeated twice or three times, with a reprise or not – those must surely have been matters that Mozart decided on the spur of the moment,' says Schmid. 'He created in the here and now. Nowadays, though, it's easy for the here and now to get lost in classical music.' And Schmid goes on to cite an example: 'Take Mozart's sonata in B-flat major, for instance, the most famous of his thirty-two violin sonatas. Well, he wrote it specifically with the violinist Regina Strinasacchi in mind, whose playing he really adored, but when it came to premiering the piece in front of Emperor Joseph II, Mozart was running so late that he hadn't managed to write down the piano part. So he just went ahead and played the whole sonata off the top of his head. At that stage, the only part that existed was for the violin, so he must have had an amazing talent for improvising,' enthuses the violin virtuoso, before adding: 'That's what really connects me to Mozart. When there's no score to work from any more, I can still keep on playing.'

Schmid also believes that Mozart and Salzburg have made him what he is. Born in Vienna, he came to Salzburg at the age of seven. 'Naturally, you get typecast if you grow up here, where it's all about Mozart. Anyone who shows any talent as a kid and shows that they've got music in their blood instantly gets sneered at as a little Mozart.' His father, who was a real Mozart aficionado, introduced him to the master's oeuvre at an early stage. 'In actual fact, I felt marooned in Salzburg, my parents had to move here and for the first few years I was really unhappy, but now I've made my peace with the city,' he explains. Yet his heart remained in Vienna, he admits. And does he feel a connection to Mozart? Yes, and at least that had helped him retain a critical perspective on Salzburg, since as a travelling artiste he was forced to spend plenty of time away from the city.

Benjamin Schmid can understand why Thomas Bernhard was so rude about the place. He believes his rejection resulted from 'love, his uncompromising nature and his burning need to be loved. And his love went unrequited; that was often the case with Mozart too. Bernhard worked through that disappointment over and over again by launching vitriolic attacks.' And he adds: 'Fact is, what he says is all true. This yearning to be a more aesthetically minded and intelligent place, and its narrow-mindedness.'

Schmid takes care not to perform too frequently in Salzburg himself. 'I'm constantly having to stop myself from doing things.' Like Hank, he's disappointed that jazz doesn't get much of a look-in here. For seventeen years, the autumn jazz festival organised by Johannes Kunz had managed to fill the festival hall with jazz. 'That was a great achievement,' he says, but it's all in the past now. He sees his appearances at the series of free-entry events called 'Jazz and the City' as more like a visit to the pub, not the big-concert experience he's accustomed to. And in any case he fights shy of performing Mozart here for fear of becoming jaded. 'There have been instances where people have called their entire stage performing career into question because they've had to play "Eine kleine Nachtmusik" too many times and at some point decide they just can't take it any longer. All of that goes on in Salzburg.'

So he puts all his energies into the Mozarteum, his 'epicentre', where he has returned to teach and where everything, from the Café Bazar to his violin maker, is within easy walking distance. In order to perform his concerts all round the world, he needs to be 'musically grounded', as he puts it, a feeling he gets from the local folk music and all the other things that have their roots here, Mozart included.

Sabina Hank finishes her second cappuccino; she needs to be off again. She loves her native city. When it's empty, 'it really rocks', but that doesn't happen very often. Only in the evenings. She needs her peace and quiet, so she's moved out to the countryside, to a small mountain village with barely a couple of dozen houses. 'No one bothers about jazz there. The neighbours know I'm a musician, but they're interested in me as Sabina.' It's different in the city.

'No,' she says after a long pause for thought, 'The Salzburg city-dwellers just aren't as down-to-earth and straight as that, no question. It's a town and country thing, like the opening scene in *The Sound of Music*.'

3

A Metropolis for a Few Weeks

The hub of the world and a longing for peace and quiet

Y OU DON'T HAVE TO GO BACK as far as 1822, when
Emperor Franz I held a reception for his Russian counterpart Czar Alexander I in Salzburg: that was just a one-day
event, then they were gone. All the same, it was a state visit
that the world took note of – albeit without any television
cameras back then. These were certainly present, though,
when US president Gerald Ford fell down the steps of Air
Force One. He was in Salzburg on a flying visit, and the
images of his mishap went round the world. Harry Truman
had gone there before him, while Richard Nixon visited the
city as vice president in 1956 and then returned as president
in 1972, staying for three days. In the meantime, various other
dignitaries made whistle-stop tours to the city of Mozart,
including the Shah of Persia, Nikita Khrushchev, and Queen
Frederica of Greece. Queen Elizabeth II also stayed here for
one night in 1969. In the seventies, they came thick and fast.
King Hussein of Jordan paid a visit, the Egyptian president

Anwar el-Sadat came several times, and the city also hosted the presidents of Zambia, Tunisia and Senegal. Queen Margrethe II of Denmark arrived on 5 April 1979, but left again shortly after. These fleeting visits made headlines, even in the international press. Margaret Thatcher was a complete exception in this respect; in 1984, the British prime minister came to attend the Salzburg Festival and stayed for a whole twelve days, making a second visit – this time for ten days – the following year. In 1988, the city hosted a three-day visit by Pope John Paul II, while two years later Presidents Václav Havel of Czechoslovakia and Richard von Weizsäcker of Germany held a two-day summit here. The long list includes the Norwegian royal couple, the king of Belgium and many others. From around 2005 onwards, high-ranking visitors became a bit thinner on the ground, though those who did come were no less prominent than before. VIPs came from China, Thailand and Portugal. And on every occasion, Salzburg was in the full glare of the world's press for one or maybe two days before peace returned once more.

Salzburg knows all about being in the spotlight one day and out of it the next. Briefly a metropolis – and then a little provincial town again.

'It's nice for us Salzburgers when we get to play at being the hub of the world. But I won't lie to you – we're also delighted when we're left to our own devices again,' says Helga Rabl-Stadler, president of the Salzburg Festival committee. She announces this quite publicly, at a reception to mark the opening of the festival season, though admittedly only to an audience of native Salzburgers. After all, no one wants to appear unfriendly to guests.

It's impossible to imagine a more candid expression of the inhabitants' ambivalent attitude to the many visitors who come here. This is the permanent mental state of a place that aspires to be a world city while at the same time being a martyr to this goal. Does it really want that status? Rabl-Stadler's predecessor, Heinrich Wiesmüller, isn't so sure about that. 'Of course, we're not a real world city, but we play at being one, and the guests who come here gamely play along. And they're amazed at how many people there are here and start to believe that we really are very significant,' he once said, also quite publicly, on television. The entire city is a stage. The spotlight comes on, and goes off again. Silence, please, and ... action!

There's no getting round it; every year, in summer, this architectural marvel is subjected to what can only be described as an invasion. Alongside the festival visitors, who bring a lot of revenue to the city, there are also hordes of sightseeing tourists, who arrive by the coachload and only spend a very short time here. On average, visitors from Europe stay here for just under two days, while those from Asia only manage a day and a half. And on bad weather days, their numbers are swelled by people coming into the city from the surrounding holiday regions to shop. If you aren't able to spend the day by a lakeside basking in the sun, walking or playing golf, then you can simply hop in a car and take a trip to the Getreidegasse or come and enjoy a coffee at Café Tomaselli. Provided you can get into the city, that is. Nose-to-tail traffic jams are the norm on such days, and it sometimes gets so bad that the roads into Salzburg have to be completely cordoned off and the tourists ferried into the centre from the outskirts on shuttle buses.

Allegedly, there are certain guests from southern climes, from the burning sands of Arabia, who are drawn to Salzburg primarily because of the rain. For them, the infamous Salzburg *Schnürlregen* (literally 'string rain', that is, a steady soaking drizzle) is a cheap tourist attraction. Despite their name – which means 'The Bores' – the Salzburg music outfit Die Langweiler produced an upbeat little number celebrating this phenomenon:

> *Bei uns in Salzburg,*
> *da scheint die Sonne nur in Strömen,*
> *bei uns in Salzburg,*
> *da sind die Straßen immer nass,*
> *da kummt der Regen wie die Sunn,*
> *glei wird's schütten!*
> *Salzburger Schnürlregen,*
> *das einzige Kulturgut, für das ma in der Stadt*
> *ka Eintrittskarten braucht.*

[Here in Salzburg,
the sun only shines in streams,
here in Salzburg,
the streets are always wet,
here comes the rain just like the sun,

soon there'll be a downpour!
Salzburg string rain –
it's the only bit of culture in the city
you don't need to buy tickets for.]

Who knows, maybe somebody will find a way of charging for it. For the true high tourist season is only very brief: the five weeks of the festival. Even by September, things have quietened down. Many shops and restaurants close out of sheer exhaustion for a couple of weeks after the summer season. This is when restaurateurs and those who are weary of the festival take a break. And lo and behold, some people then start complaining that the city has too little to offer outside the festival period. They reckon 'something should be going on' all year round. Ideally, twelve months of the festival. 'Salzburg simply couldn't take it,' the senior tourist manager for the city, Herbert Brugger, maintains. 'Even a city needs a bit of peace and quiet sometimes, like in February, when it's got time to pause and catch its breath, clear up and get ready for the next season.'

In Leopoldskron Palace, which was home to the theatre director Max Reinhardt for eighteen years and the place where he came up with the idea of the festival, as well as being where *The Sound of Music* was shot and where Karl Lagerfeld staged one of the best and most expensive fashion shows ever (an extravaganza that was filmed and shown all round the world), even the sitting president of the festival committee won't have any truck with the idea of a year-round festival. It is almost like that even now. There's Mozart Week in January, to mark the maestro's birthday. Recently, this has been rechristened the 'Winter Festival Season'. Then, at Easter, Christian Thielemann, one of the most charismatic directors working today, heads up the Easter Festival. At Whitsun, the opera singer Cecilia Bartoli – Rabl-Stadler calls her 'the signal rocket for the Whitsun Festival' – pulls out all the stops. Then there's the main summer festival, and in the autumn it's jazz, followed by the Advent Singing Festival – another major audience magnet – or alternatively the winter festival for circus performance.

'I warned against putting too much strain on this small town,' Rabl-Stadler says, 'but we've got such a wide range of brands that are known worldwide that we run the risk of neglecting a proper brand development. From "Silent Night" to *The Sound of Music*. Certainly, in the case of Mozart there was a danger of leaving him to the Viennese until it dawned on us that he only died there and that we should be playing up the fact that this was his birthplace!' And so in 2006, the 250th anniversary of Mozart's birth, defying all the gloomy prognostications, the city staged every single one of his twenty-two operas and in the process regained air supremacy over Mozart. For the city, the old marketing adage of playing to one's strengths meant deliberately focusing on the theme of music, she says, fully conscious that by now some other art forms feel discriminated against by this decision. 'Music drowns out everything else here,' she admits. In economic terms, too. The budget of the world's greatest festival stands at sixty million euros. Even in the absence of any advertising, visitors flock here from seventy-four countries, thirty-five of them outside Europe. 'That makes it much easier to bring international sponsors on board; other art forms have a harder time of it,' she concedes. For within Salzburg itself, there are only a very few large companies with sponsorship potential.

Business requires more favourable conditions for industrial companies to invest here, she continues. That brings jobs, which after all is the only thing that secures people's livelihoods. And the universities don't feel that they get enough support. Despite there being more than 20,000 students here, Salzburg is not very well known or recognised as a university town. Salzburg really ought to become an educational capital, she claims. Others insist that Salzburg should position itself as a conference and trade-fair centre. The city's restaurant and hospitality sector, meanwhile, wants above all to see all-year-round occupancy. A steady flow of visitors, drawn by constant attractions. The city should always be full, but not overfull.

Sure, the city lives on tourists and even likes them (to a certain degree, anyhow), but sometimes it finds itself stifled by them. The irregular pulse of the influxes of visitors has become a logistical problem. Little wonder, then, that repeated attempts are made to make the eleven months when the main festival isn't on more attractive and so distribute the influx more evenly.

Certain things have already been done to change the

cityscape in this regard. In order to not simply appear like some Baroque open-air museum, the private Salzburg Foundation has over the past ten years invited a succession of internationally renowned artists to create works for public spaces. The clear intention was to stir up debate. The first piece to be installed was by Anselm Kiefer, who erected a pavilion in Furtwängler Park. Sixty books cast in lead, Moroccan thorn bushes and rolls of NATO barbed wire play on the idea of the transience of time. Yet the most photographed public artwork is undoubtedly the 9-metre-high sculpture *Sphaera* by Stephan Balkenhol on the Kapitelplatz, a large golden ball surmounted by the figure of a man calmly gazing at the fortress. The artist who stirred up the most controversy, though, was Markus Lüpertz with his *Homage to Mozart*, which was installed outside St Mark's, a Baroque church designed by Fischer von Erlach. Not everyone liked the bronze figure, least of all the self-appointed moral guardian of Austria, Martin Humer, who considered it a pornographic work. In front of TV cameras, he proceeded summarily to daub it with red and green oil paint and plaster it with white goose-down feathers. He justified his intervention by announcing 'At least I can make a Papageno out of the hideous thing', though his actions only succeeded in giving huge publicity to the Mozart sculpture. The matter subsequently came to court; Humer was found guilty of causing criminal damage, though he himself didn't end up tarred and feathered.

For arty types who want to take in all these modern pieces of sculpture, there's a separate city tour running from Anthony Cragg's work on the Makartplatz to Christian Boltanski's *Vanitas* in the choir crypt of the cathedral. Public space is a quintessential feature of a Baroque city. It is unclear how many of the one and a half million tourists who visit Salzburg each year come specifically to view its art and architecture. One certain statistic is that the Summer Festival 'generates' some 340,000 overnight stays. And in any event, after Vienna, the city on the Salzach indisputably occupies the number two spot in Austrian city tourism. Although the metropolis on the Danube accounts for two-thirds of all overnight stays by guests in Austria, Salzburg is much more compact, so visitors are far less likely to go astray here than in the former imperial capital.

Cheap flights and internet booking have made city breaks a year-round phenomenon nowadays, and this kind of stay doesn't even necessarily require any great cultural highlights. Salzburg's twelve thousand beds are slept in by two and a half million guests annually, and on top of this there are another six million day visitors who only stay for a few hours taking photos and perhaps doing a bit of shopping before departing once more. For many in Salzburg, that's too many visitors. Even those whose livelihood is tourism mostly only desire one thing as private individuals: peace, tranquillity, and then some more peace.

So a lot of moaning goes on in Salzburg, about too few or too many visitors. 'Salzburgers are real moaners, only not as original as the ones in Vienna,' the festival president says with a grin. 'And Austrians in general are a strange mix of hubris and an inferiority complex. But only in Salzburg does that have the effect of making us think that we are the hub of the world, but then we're suddenly beset by doubt and start worrying that we're actually too small for all of this.'

This city doesn't overstretch itself by repeatedly standing in the spotlight for a brief spell. Nor does it overstretch itself by being the world's premier city of music for a short while, or by being overrun on a daily basis by people intent on taking thousands of selfies.

Perhaps the only way it overstretches itself is by constantly wanting to be something other than it is.

4

Hiya, Anna!

Nowhere else can you run across
Anna Netrebko so easily as in Salzburg

Y OU COULDN'T HOPE to find a bridge with a name
more supportive of the state than one called simply the
Staatsbrücke ('State Bridge'). Granted, that actually makes
it sound a bit highfalutin, as if it were some vital lifeline for
the state. It certainly isn't that, though it is for the city. There
has been some form of crossing at this point for a thousand
years, linking the north and the south bank of the Salzach.
With previous structures having been swept away many
times by floods, the current bridge is the tenth to stand at
this spot, and it is the crossing between parts of the old city
that has been used by innumerable official state visitors to the
country. For most of them stay at the Hotel Sacher, which in
former times – also very patriotically – bore the name 'Österreichischer Hof' (Hotel Austria).

This is the city's grandest hotel, the counterpart of the
Imperial in Vienna. Hillary Clinton stayed here in 1997,

without her husband Bill but accompanied by her daughter Chelsea, as did Prince Charles with his then-unmarried partner Lady Camilla Parker Bowles. Likewise Margaret Thatcher, Romano Prodi and Richard von Weizsäcker, along with many world-renowned artists. But no matter how prominent the guests, they always appreciate the personal touch from their hosts.

So you'll often find Elisabeth Gürtler down here by the banks of the Salzach, especially in summer, even though she has already handed over the running of the hotel to her children. Dressed in a smart black suit, she sits at a little table facing the bar, sipping her tea with lemon and telling tales of former times. As MD of the Vienna-based Sacher hospitality empire, she took over the Österreichischer Hof in Salzburg in 1990 and ten years later rechristened it the Hotel Sacher. Members of the real establishment and the genuinely wealthy aren't ever remotely difficult or demanding, she says with a smile. 'The most problematic people are those who can only just afford to stay here. Those who have only recently had their first sniff of luxury can't get enough of it, and they find fault with everything.' This sometimes results in heated arguments about whether the window of their room is 'only' facing the Kapuzinerberg rather than affording them a view of the fortress. Other hotels simply don't have that choice and yet still manage to accommodate plenty of VIPs. Take the Hotel Schloss Mönchstein, for example, which is at the top of the high-end hospitality sector and also literally on top of the Mönchsberg, in a location that is rather tucked away and far more discreet than the Sacher's. Or the 600-year-old 'high-class guesthouse', the Goldener Hirsch in the Getrei-degasse. This is the haunt of the aristocracy. 'In their mind's eye they can still see the figure of its former owner Count Johannes Walderdorff in his lederhosen,' Gürtler says, and muses admiringly on how this great, gangly figure was able in his day to lure guests like Princess Caroline of Monaco and Queen Sofia of Spain to his establishment. But also Luciano Pavarotti and Thomas Gottschalk. And Romy Schneider, who also had a soft spot for the new Sacher.

The prominently positioned Sacher benefited greatly from the patronage of official state visitors. It's impossible to miss the flags on the roof, proclaiming its national significance far and wide. During the World Economic Forum in 1997, the hotel played host to six or seven heads of state, and generally speaking it was true that the Austrian president at the time, Thomas Klestil, did much to raise the international profile of Salzburg, Gürtler says.

Nowadays, state visits are rather sober working affairs. The security barriers hinder normal operations. Yet even so, things still aren't always in dead earnest. When Elisabeth Gürtler was escorting the Romanian president Ion Iliescu to his suite, her dog ran up the stairs after her – and promptly leapt up onto the bed right in front of the state visitor. 'That was incredibly embarrassing,' she admits, adding that the memory still makes her cringe even now. By contrast, her recollections of the visit of the Dalai Lama in June 1998 are nothing but happy ones: 'When the orange-robed members of his entourage used to pace around the corridors at six in the morning meditating, it conjured up a mystical atmosphere all its own.'

Admittedly, it's not always the case that the Schwarzstraße in front of the hotel is jammed with limousines with flashing blue lights and police escorts. Politicians increasingly have to weigh up whether they can justify to their electorates the expense of staying at a luxury hotel. Movie stars are exempt from this kind of criticism. Her eyes glistening with pride, Elisabeth Gürtler then proceeds to show me the wall of photos in the lobby. Renée Fleming, Dianne Reeves, Dee Dee Bridgewater, Telly Savalas and Tom Hanks have all left signed pictures of themselves here, as have Kent Nagano, Cecilia Bartoli and Udo Jürgens from the world of music. There are no demarcations between genres in a hotel. In the adjoining café you can still see a picture labelled 'Princess Grace of Monaco, 1965' and above it one signed ostentatiously 'Best wishes, Plácido Domingo'. The greatest prize, however, is the guest book, gilt-edged but otherwise rather nondescript in appearance. Even so, all the good and the great who have visited are immortalised there. The hotel's safe is the fitting tabernacle for this volume.

Any VIPs who happen to be in Salzburg in mid-August can be found at the Mushroom Banquet at the Sacher. Assuming they've been invited, that is! Elisabeth Gürtler inaugurated this tradition as a sit-down meal. To begin with, it was just for sixty people, until ever-increasing demand saw it expand to fill the whole of the hotel's dining space. For days, rumours would buzz around town as to who would be seated in which room and at what table next to which other guests – or not, as the case may be. However, their children have rather shunned this method of ranking high society and those Salzburgers who were permitted to hobnob with it, and they now only uphold the tradition in the form of a flying lunch. There's no longer any formal seating arrangement, but as the grande dame of the establishment herself admits, perhaps that makes people a bit more communicative.

Besides, to achieve the much-sought-after aim of rubbing shoulders with celebrities of stage and screen you don't actually require an invitation to the Sacher nowadays – still less, as was once the case, to the even more exclusive lunches hosted by 'Mammarazza' in Fuschl. For thirty-five years, Countess Marianne zu Sayn-Wittgenstein-Sayn, who was generally known simply as 'Manni' and who could usually be found out and about with her camera snapping prominent Salzburgers, ennobled all those she considered 'the right sort of people' with lunch invitations to her garden. Her guests included Gunter Sachs, Sean Connery and Arnold Schwarzenegger.

But even those who are not the right sort aren't totally out of the picture where VIP-watching in Salzburg is concerned. To be sure, during extended stays here rehearsing or performing the stars tend to prefer living in rented houses some way out of the city, where they can enjoy more privacy. On the other hand, though, it's not uncommon to run into them somewhere in the festival quarter. Most likely in a little pub-restaurant in the Wiener Philharmonikergasse, there in a corner where, unnoticed by most people, the little triangle that gives the place its name – Restaurant Triangel – hangs. With seating for just fifty-five people, it can sometimes get a tad snug in here; only the summer months present no problem, as everyone crowds onto the many outdoor tables. It's just that the waiters have got a lot more ground to cover then.

One such waiter is Alexander Holzer, who's been at the pub for ten years and is the owner's right-hand man. The landlord is called Franz. That's how everyone knows him. It's neither here nor there that his surname's Gensbichler. Franz *is* The Triangle, and its reputation and his are one and the same. They're both straightforward, down-to-earth and no-frills, just like the menu here. Where possible, Franz sources all his produce from the local region, and the drinks he serves are Salzburg-brewed beer, good Austrian wine and spirits – no Coca-Cola or Red Bull.

'This simplicity really appeals to artists in particular, because it means they're left in peace and treated like normal human beings,' explains Alexander. That makes sense – since they come and go here all the time, they're not rare exotic creatures like in other establishments. The familiar 'Du' form of address is used in The Triangle, reminiscent of the cama-raderie among strangers who find themselves atop a high mountain peak. Even the performers are addressed in this way. 'I say "Hiya" or "Hello" to Anna too,' Alexander says, referring to the Russian soprano Anna Netrebko, who often drops in here when she's in Salzburg, arriving either on foot

or by bike. 'And even if the former chancellor Franz Vranitzky were to stop by, then I'd say "How d'you do" to him
too – not that that's my normal way of greeting people,' he
adds after a short pause. Vranitzky isn't someone who looks
like he'd tolerate a waiter calling him 'Du'. But that's clearly
not the case with a genuine diva.

Even so, politicians are quite frequent visitors here too.
'The former German president Roman Herzog comes in at
least once or twice a year. And Minister of Culture Oster-
mayer was here in the summer.' And what about church
leaders? 'I've never seen the archbishop in here, either the
current or the previous one, but the new abbot of St Peter's
often turns up.' His monastery, the oldest in the city and in
the whole of the German-speaking world, is virtually next
door, no further away than the festival theatre.

Because the pub is part of the estate of the Archdiocese of
Salzburg, it runs a kind of 'refectory' for students at lunch-
time by offering a cut-price midday menu. Nevertheless, The
Triangle is by no means a student pub. Performers lend it a
touch of pizzazz: actors, singers, musicians and conductors,
from Barenboim to Thielemann. The walls are crammed with
photographs and autographed cards. Most of them are dedicated to the landlord Franz. On one, René Pape expresses his
gratitude. 'To my dearest friend,' writes Michael Schade, and
adds: 'I'd go home if it wasn't for you.' 'Impossible to imagine
Salzburg without you!' proclaims Angelika Kirchschlager's
speech bubble. Alongside are dedications from Mojca
Erdmann, Barbara Bonney and Nina Hoss. 'My thanks to

The Triangle,' writes Max Raabe. Gaby Dohm looks forward to 'the next bash,' while Jonas Kaufmann's contribution reads 'Singer dreaming of his first beer in The Triangle'. Some of the photos bear witness to wild nights in the hostelry. Pride of place goes to a large poster showing Rolando Villazón. On occasion, Franz will order a round of drinks on the house in honour of his guests. 'The boss is a very generous guy,' says Alexander.

The frequent matinee performances of the Salzburg Festival's most famous annual production, Hugo von Hofmannsthal's *Jedermann* (*Everyman*), enable cast members and their hangers-on to become pretty much regular fixtures at the pub on summer evenings. 'Simonischek comes in here a lot, along with Ofczarek, Obonya, the directors and the whole crew. Birgit Minichmayr and Ben Becker have often come along too, and it's not unheard of for the booze to flow rather freely,' he confides. Evidently Jonas Kaufmann and Rolando Villazón are more discreet regulars. 'They're absolutely charming,' he reveals, his eyes aglow.

At that point, as if appearing on his cue in *Everyman*, the Salzburg actor and cabaret artist Fritz Egger walks in. He's just been shopping at the fruit and veg market on nearby Universitätsplatz and felt the urge to swing by his local for a quick beer. He sometimes goes to Resch & Lieblich in the Toscaninihof as well. At one time, when Peter Stein was the artistic director of the festival, that was *the* place for artistes to hang out, he recounts. But that pub is tucked away and even smaller than The Triangle. Here you can always be sure of running into someone. You can see everybody who's anybody here. And – not an unimportant consideration in Salzburg – it's also somewhere where you can be seen. That's the saving grace of the place, and something that Franz has capitalised upon. At festival time in the high summer, on every performance day, two tables are automatically reserved for the *Everyman* cast and crew. Egger, who has played the part of the Debtor for several years now, frequently takes advantage of this facility, recuperating here from the blistering heat of the open-air stage on the cathedral square, after he has finished vainly imploring the wealthy Everyman to write off his debt. 'Besides, actors are sociable people at the best of times,' he says by way of explaining the enduring popularity of the pub among the thespian fraternity.

The waiter brings a second beer. I ask him whether he often gets to see his famous guests performing. 'No, never,' Alexander replies, 'that's our busy period, so I don't have the time.' And if he or one of the other waiters finds himself free of an evening, they don't go to the Festival Hall. 'The tickets are expensive, and you can't get hold of them in any case,' he explains, only to immediately contradict himself: 'Of course, there'd be ways and means of getting tickets, given that we know them all. But I never do.'

So these two worlds – that of artists and that of waiters – remain apart. They come into contact over schnitzels and beer, but they never merge, despite being closer to one another here than in any other city, and closer in The Triangle than in any other pub. The two groups are on familiar

'Du' terms – but still they stay at arm's length from one another. Nonetheless, there is probably no other pub in the world with such a high incidence of relaxed encounters with singers, actors, directors and musicians, or with this unique mix of performers and stagehands, politicians and captains of industry, theatre-goers and students.

Sure, performers in New York, Milan or Vienna also have locals that they like to frequent, in the vicinity of the Met, around La Scala, or near the Staatsoper. But there it's a much more diffuse business. In so far as they are recognised at all, they stick out as stars among the general populace. Here they no longer attract special attention, because you're constantly running into them. Yet at the same time, there's an instant recognition factor precisely because of that. On stage, on the street, in hotels or at the next table.

That's the peculiarity of a festival that outshines everything else in a city of very manageable proportions.

5

The Power of Piety

*There were no half-measures when the city's former
rulers built the landmarks it's famous for today*

I T IS THE year 2416. The sleek supersonic airliner has just
disgorged a small tour group from Europe at an airport ter-
minal in the Middle East. Their aim is to visit Aleppo, a city
with a great history. Roman ruins lie beneath the imposing
buildings there, which are barely 400 years old. Back then,
following a civil war that dragged on for years, the city began
to flourish once more. Reconstruction was funded by subter-
ranean bounty in the form of oil. A succession of Islamic dic-
tators had older buildings that displeased them demolished
in order to create a city that has since become a magnet for
admirers from all round the world. A panorama of mosques
and palaces. The human lives that were sacrificed to achieve
all this counted for nothing.

Even back then, from 2006 on, Aleppo had been, after
Mecca, the second most important capital of Islamic culture.
Christians lived there too, but Muslims were in the majority

and, as adherents of different branches of Islam, they became embroiled in an exhausting power struggle. The Shiites, who held power at the time and were allied with the neighbouring fellow Shiite countries of Iraq and Iran, were sworn enemies of the Sunnis, by far the largest branch of Islam worldwide, whose principal power base lay in Saudi Arabia. Shiites repeatedly displaced Sunnis and vice versa. At some stage, much later, they returned and lived alongside each other, and then cheek-by-jowl with one another, and eventually became reconciled, to the extent that it no longer mattered which branch of the faith a person professed. Now, in 2416, what was still taken as read even a couple of hundred years before – namely that the political elites came exclusively from the centres of religious power – is simply inconceivable. An Islamic Enlightenment effectively decoupled the institutions of state and religion.

A fairy tale? Or just a transposition of the actual facts?

There are Roman ruins beneath the current city of Salzburg. Using mineral wealth, in this instance gold from the Hohe Tauern mountain range and salt from the Dürrnberg near Hallein, dictatorial prince-archbishops funded the construction of a series of magnificent buildings. Citizens' houses were simply demolished to make way for the vast cathedral and various Baroque squares. After Rome, Salzburg was the second most powerful centre of Catholicism. Anything that wasn't Catholic was destroyed. In the late seventeenth century and during the great wave of expulsions after 1732, all Protestants were driven from the country.

Thousands upon thousands of them, mercilessly and with no legal redress. Anyone who refused was tortured and executed by being beheaded, drowned or burned alive. Sometimes, they were 'merely' forced into submission by being made to undergo mock executions. Such was the face of Christian brotherly love prior to the Western Enlightenment. Jesuits who were specially brought into Austria honed their skills in heresy trials. Archbishop Firmian allied himself with Catholic Bavaria and Tyrol, which promptly closed their borders to Protestants trying to flee. The appointment of archbishops, elevated from the nobility and elected by the cathedral chapter, was rubber-stamped by the Pope, but even so these individuals were intent on pleasing the Pontiff and showing him a Salzburg that was as Catholic as it could possibly be.

The visible trappings of power were thus already in place. The prince-archbishops Wolf Dietrich von Raitenau, Markus Sittikus and Paris von Lodron were the prime movers in developing the cityscape that is so greatly admired today. From the late sixteenth century onwards, they brought in architects from outside the city, mostly from Italy or from elsewhere in Austria, such as Vincenzo Scamozzi and Fischer von Erlach.

For Wolf Dietrich, it was a stroke of good fortune that a fire razed the city's old medieval cathedral to the ground in 1598. That was the fourth time that a church on the site had burnt down, so Dietrich did not remotely need to pay homage to the cathedral's original founder, the abbot-bishop Virgil, when planning a replacement. So without further ado he had the remains of the previous structure cleared away, along with fifty-five dwellings. Vincenzo Scamozzi's first plan envisaged a cathedral almost the size of St Peter's in Rome, with its main entrance on the Residenzplatz. Although that design proved too expensive, the structure that arose was still an imposing 101 metres in length. Around it, a whole new city quarter was laid out, including the Hofstall, the Griesgasse, the Franziskanergasse and the archbishop's palace immediately adjacent to the cathedral, while on the opposite bank of the Salzach, the castle that later became Mirabell was built to house his mistress and their fifteen children. The immediate result was economic ruin. Wolf Dietrich was arrested and paid for his folly by spending the rest of his days incarcerated in the Hohensalzburg Fortress.

However, his fate did not daunt those who came after him. Construction was resumed in spite of the ongoing Thirty Years' War; the only change was that subsequent archbishops shied away from the same degree of excess. Even so, Markus Sittikus also built himself a summer residence in Hellbrunn, south of the Mönchsberg. It's a magnificent, lavish and playful edifice; the ornamental fountains in its grounds still enthral people now. Salzburg kept itself out of the war by supplying arms, and in any case the Swedes considered the fortress impregnable. And it's true, it never was overrun. Even nowadays, it still boasts a number of sumptuous princely chambers, fitted out for the rulers to take refuge in. In the shadow of the fortress, one magnificent building after another sprang up. With the Counter Reformation, the

Catholic Church was intent on demonstrating its power, in defiance of the example of the Franciscans. This mendicant order of monks was the ecclesiastical counterpoint to the burgeoning might of the Church in the Baroque. They still provide soup kitchens for beggars in the city today. All the same, their Gothic-Romanesque church in Salzburg does not come across as understated. It is linked directly to the palace via a walkway high above the heads of the common people, naturally.

The density of churches in comparison with the number of inhabitants is as great in Salzburg's Old Town as it is in Rome. The oldest of them is St Michael's Church, which is situated between the Waagplatz and the Residenzplatz and whose foundations date back to the time of the Carolingians. It's a miracle that it survived the prince-archbishops' mania for new building during the Baroque period. Granted, it was refurbished several times. As was the Franciscan Church, whose original Gothic spire was trimmed down because it was higher than the cathedral. The medieval Gothic church of St Nicholas in the Kaigasse did not fare so well, however. Prince-Archbishop Wolf Dietrich von Raitenau had it demolished and completely rebuilt in the Baroque manner. It is now a residential building.

Rome was always the model for Salzburg. St Peter's Abbey was founded on the complex of burial caves and early Christian rock churches here: the catacombs. The process that began under the monks Rupert and Virgil really took off later. Around 1700, the St Cajetan Church was completed.

However, Prince-Archbishop Johann Ernst von Thun kept architect Giovanni Gaspare Zuccalli waiting for his payment, having at around the same time also commissioned the Collegiate Church, which was consecrated just a couple of years later. This latter place of worship, planned during the rule of Paris von Lodron, was eventually built by Fischer von Erlach and is a grandiose affair, and indeed the same thing can be said of all four churches in Salzburg that are based on his designs. In around 1770, a plan to replicate the city walls of Rome was put forward. This piece of gigantomania would only be surpassed by the Nazis' plan to site a huge forum complete with military garrison headquarters, festival theatre and arena on the Kapuzinerberg. Certain architectural schemes were thwarted by history, while opposition from residents managed to see off others, such as the idea proposed in 1900 to pull down the long-disused fortress and use the rubble to control the flow of the Salzach.

Certainly, no one attempted to challenge the visible power of the Church. It was only in 1803, as a result of the secularisation that followed the French Revolution and the Napoleonic Wars, that the ecclesiastical princes were divested of their worldly power. Salzburg became an electorate and soon after a duchy. And it was 1951 before the incumbent prince-archbishop Andreas Rohracher renounced this splendid but long since meaningless title. All the same, Salzburg's special position in canon law vis-à-vis Rome remains in full force to this day.

At the First Vatican Council of 1869–70, Pope Pius IX

referred to the Archbishop of Salzburg as the 'half-Pope'. Not without reason, since a warrant of 1027 issued by Pope John XIX authorised the Archbishop of Salzburg to act in cases of emergency as the Pope's proxy in the region north of the Alps and even empowered him to appoint bishops. As an autonomous representative of the Pope, the *Legatus natus*, or 'born envoy', was entitled to ride on a horse decked out in red and to wear the legate's purple apparel when performing all his official duties, even beyond the bounds of his own province.

Nowadays nobody goes around on horseback, but the cardinal's purple is still worn, and the title *Legatus natus* also lives on, alongside that of *Primus Germaniae* ('Primate of the German Lands'). He officially ranks above all the other bishops in the German-speaking realm, but he has no jurisdiction over them.

Not that the powerful old princes of the Church were ever much loved among the general populace. 'Salzburgers are more ecclesiastically curious than pious and are always prepared to prosecute their bishops,' the historian Franz Martin wrote in the 1950s. This resentment evaporated as the Church's power waned, but people around here still aren't particularly devout, at least no more or less than in other cities, explains the priest and art historian Johannes Neuhardt. Now well into his eighties, Neuhardt was formerly dean of the cathedral and a member of its chapter, which entitled him to vote in the election of bishops. 'The largest Catholic cities in mainland Europe are now Paris, Rome and Vienna. And the majority of practising Catholics are in Vienna. If it weren't for the tourists, you could forget Rome,' he harshly announces. So, nowadays Salzburg is better placed statistically than Rome.

Since Vatican I, however, Salzburg's independence from Rome has been severely curtailed. The cathedral chapter no longer has complete freedom of action but instead has to choose from three candidates for bishop put forward by the Pope. And it has sometimes been necessary for the cathedral chapter to simply choke back its anger and opt for the best of three bad alternatives. The Catholic Church has proved itself capable of weathering such storms; after all, it still thinks on a timescale of centuries.

6

The Dark Side of the Crags

Backdrop to the city and the theatre

NOT ALL THE CONSTRUCTION PROJECTS that the princes of the Church commissioned were in the service of self-indulgence or symbolically projecting their power. Cutting a passage through the Mönchsberg was a milestone in the city's development. The 135-metre-long tunnel was completed in 1766 and the entrance on the Old Town side, between the Pferdeschwemme ('Horse Bath') and the Festival Hall, was adorned with an ornamental façade known as the Sigmundstor.

Seventy years earlier, Fischer von Erlach had demonstrated that the conglomerate rock from which the Mönchsberg is composed could be successfully worked when his plans to convert a former quarry into a riding school were successfully realised. Ninety-six boxes from where onlookers could watch equestrian training were hewn out of the rock face and a tower was erected above. Today the arcades of the 'riding school in the hillside' (*Felsenreitschule*) make up an enormous performance arena, whose 40-metre-wide stage presents directors with considerable challenges. Max Reinhardt was the first to try and tackle these challenges with his 1926 production of Goldoni's *The Servant of Two Masters*.

The adjacent crags form the brooding backdrop to the whole of the city's Old Town quarter. They are menacing and protective at the same time. At certain points, to enhance its role as a defensive barrier, the steep cliff face has been artificially smoothed off to create a sheer vertical wall. In other cases, these precipitous drops were brought about by rockfalls, which often claimed many lives. In 1669, for instance, many people were entombed inside their houses in the Gstättengasse when a section of the cliff gave way. In an attempt to avert such disasters, every year thereafter in spring the escarpment has been cleared of loose rocks by hand. The mountain cleaners, a group of around a dozen audacious men, abseil down the cliff and dangle there on their ropes chipping off unstable bits of rock and clearing away dangerous plant roots that might precipitate a larger rockfall. Each spring, as they work their way along the cliff in their blue overalls, yellow safety helmets and red climbing harnesses, they become a tourist attraction in their own right.

Fear of this craggy spine of rock in the centre of the city persists to this day. Or at least a healthy respect. Salzburg has learned to live with the crags. Although some people are intent on dying there, it's true. It's often claimed that Salzburg has the highest suicide rate in the whole of Austria. That isn't actually true. But many of those who do not want to wait for a natural end to their days choose to hurl themselves from these precipices. In the main, it's men, and most of them choose a spot where they won't land on a house or a car roof below. The Humboldt Terrace, where the path around the Mönchsberg runs close to the edge, is one such place. Below this lies an area of hard granite paving. The course of the Salzach is very close by, and beyond it you get a panoramic view of the city in all its glory. Mirabell Palace is directly opposite at this point. You couldn't find a more theatrical location at which to take your final leave of a city.

The media no longer report such incidents, with good reason: the last thing they want to do is to lend impetus to people who are on the brink of deciding to end it all. Paramedics and undertakers dread having to retrieve bodies from here. This is the darkest side of the Salzburg crags. Wolf Haas also described this place in his best-selling novel *Silentium!*, albeit with a question mark over whether his deceased protagonist really did choose to depart this life there voluntarily.

Other places, by contrast, are positively teeming with life. The high plateau is a favourite recreational spot, a sanctuary for flora and fauna. Chamois can be found only on the Kapuzinerberg, and a marksman is employed by the city to cull them every now and then so as to keep their numbers in check. On the Mönchsberg, though, the only thing shooting down to the valley is water. At the point where the plateau transitions to the outcrop housing the fortress in the form of a saddle, the centuries-old watercourse known as the Almkanal makes its grand entrance. From here, tunnels dating from the early Middle Ages carry fresh alpine water down into the valley towards the Old Town as far as St Peter's Abbey, where it divides into seven separate channels and flows into the Salzach. This resource has had many purposes, being used not only for drinking water but also to drive mill wheels and as a cooling system for the Festival Hall. It is a truly vital artery. But it's also a leisure amenity. In its upper reaches, the stream is used as a bathing place, despite the iciness of the water, while the strong current near the Meder-Weg has even tempted a few people to surf the Alm. After all, there's got to be some compensation for the fact that Salzburg isn't by the seaside.

7

Salzburg is not Salzburg

And not all Salzburgers are Salzburgers. At least not always

THE DISTANCE FROM New York to Salzburg is pretty
much exactly 450 kilometres as the crow flies. 550 kilometres by car. Well, to Saltsburg that is, to give it its correct
spelling. Saltsburg in Pennsylvania, with a population of less
than 1,000, is situated near Greenburg, which itself is hardly
a famous metropolis. Saltsburg also has a river running
through it – its counterpart of the Salzach is called the Cone-
maugh River. But there the similarities end. This Saltsburg
was founded in the eighteenth century by emigrants from
Moravia, so it doesn't have a long history. And it is only
one of several 'Salzburgs' dotted around the world. There's
another one in Romania, for instance, near the city of Sibiu
(Hermannstadt). Its Romanian name is Ocna Sibiului, and
it too has Roman roots and became prosperous in medieval
times through the mining of salt.

Germany can lay claim to no fewer than three Salzburgs.
In the Westerwald in the state of Rhineland-Palatinate a

settlement by the name of 'Salberg' was founded in 1300, and nowadays the village is home to around 250 people. In Lower Franconia, northeast of Würzburg, there is a castle called Bad Salzburg, which is now privately owned by the Gutenberg family. And in Lower Saxony in the northeast of Germany, 50 kilometres south of Hanover, there is a Salzburg that boasts a forester's lodge as its main attraction. A handful of Protestant families settled there in 1733 after being expelled from the Salzburg region by Prince-Archbishop Leopold von Firmian. Elector George II gave each family a house, two cows and six 'Morgen' of land (roughly equivalent to one and a half hectares today). However, the refugees did not want to make a complete break with their past, and so named their new home Salzburg in memory of the one they had lost.

In the Second German Empire (1871–1918), there was also a district called Salzburg in what is now France (Château-Salins in Lorraine). During the reign of the Austro-Hungarian monarchy, a village by the name of Souuvar was known as Salzburg in German, while to the east of the city of Prešov in the same region stands the castle of Solnohrad – a brigands' stronghold now reduced to ruins – which was translated as 'Salzburg'. In the Middle Ages in Latvia there was a castle called Salisburg, built by German knights. And a prison in the US state of North Carolina bore the same name.

Who on earth can tell all these Salzburgers spread around the globe apart? After all, they have major problems in this regard even in the Austrian homeland area around the Salzach. The entire surrounding region has the same name as the city! And as it transpires, the city has a somewhat inflated opinion of itself. Out of a total of 530,000 inhabitants in the whole federal state of Salzburg, barely 150,000 live in the state capital. In the mountain meadowlands, people are conditioned by the Alpine climate. They speak their minds bluntly. Town dwellers, by contrast, tend to take verbal detours. There's a mix of those two approaches in the administrative capital of the state. In the city that has the same name as the state, that is. In order to distinguish the city-dwelling Salzburgers from the country ones, the former are referred to as *Stådinger*, with an open 'å' sound that only exists in the local dialect. Even so, this distinction is still insufficient. The city continues to expand, both as a result of a slight increase in the birth rate there and thanks to immigration. So people have taken now to differentiating between native Salzburgers and incomers.

The cabaret performer Fritz Egger puts it like this: 'There are genuine Salzburgers and typical Salzburgers. The genuine ones were born here and the typical ones come from Upper Austria.' Egger is in the latter category, having been born in Schärding am Inn.

This is the truly distinguishing feature in Salzburg. You could live a long time in Salzburg and yet never become a Salzburger. At least not in the eyes of Salzburgers. Genuine, original Salzburgers have been resident here for three generations and more. All the rest are immigrants, and they remain in some measure outsiders with the right of residence. Anyone who holds high office is respected; love first needs to be earned. That can take a long time. This city at the gateway to Western Europe was always a place of great interest for the ambitious. Firms allowed managerial careers to blossom here, while the cultural environment was always a major draw anyhow, but Salzburg has also helped boost political and even ecclesiastical careers. And so it is that several prominent Salzburg figures of recent times are outsiders with no trace of Salzach DNA in their blood. Gabi Burgstaller, for instance, the state governor from 2004 to 2013, hailed from Upper Austria, while her predecessor Franz Schausberger, former Archbishop Alois Kothgasser and his successor Franz Lackner all came from Styria, as does the city's former mayor Heinz Schaden. However, Wilfried Haslauer Jr, state governor at the time of writing, and festival president Helga Rabl-Stadler are 'genuine' Salzburgers.

But in one respect, genuine and typical Salzburgers are at one: in their often lofty sense of self-esteem, quite particularly where setting themselves apart from the outside world is concerned – especially Vienna. The two cities have been part of the same nation for over 200 years, following the definitive return of Salzburg to Austria at the Treaty of Munich (1816), but you won't hear much on this score from 'headquarters'. Not willingly, anyhow. Federalism is as highly prized there as it is in the 'sacred land of the Tyrol'. Catholicism as a cheerleader for autonomy. By contrast, where internal politics are concerned, many people who live here would argue that the citizens of Salzburg are all too compliant and submissive towards their own powers that be. That too is a legacy of history. Catholicism as an instrument of subjugation.

The special position of the Prince-Archbishopric and later the Duchy of Salzburg with regard to the Papacy has repercussions that are felt even today. This status undoubtedly rubs off on Salzburgers and strengthens them. In view of this, it is astonishing that Max Reinhardt and Hugo von Hofmannsthal were able to found the festival in Salzburg. For both of them were marked out as being indelibly Viennese, and both had Jewish roots. But they truly did earn the city's love, through a mixture of patience, hard work and not least remarkable success.

So perhaps all that stuff about distinctions doesn't quite hold true after all. One thing is certain, though: neither in Saltsburg nor in Ocna Sibiului nor in Salberg do people expend remotely so much time and effort philosophising on the subject.

8

A Village Within the City

*The farmers' market and the decorous
ambience of the Linzergasse*

THE WORLD IS A VILLAGE. There you are, lying on a beach in the Maldives, and a man comes strolling by behind you whom you'd really only recognise when he's dressed in his familiar white kit back home and manipulating your tense back muscles with his golden hands. Or you're just ordering a nice piece of grilled fish in a taverna on a Greek island as a reward for having successfully made the crossing from a neighbouring island in your sailing boat in the teeth of a force eight gale, when suddenly from the next table you hear the sound of your local dialect booming at full volume through the restaurant. Does it have to be like that? Why yes; there's just no getting round the fact that the world's a village.

And it's all the more true that a city suburb can be one as well. There, anonymity is relative, given that one is constantly running into the same people, and much is familiar. So what is a village? A sense of home, a place of manageable size. A world unto itself, containing everything that a person needs. A shop and a pub, a church and a cemetery, a main square and backyards, a school and a police station. At least, that used to be the case, before villages became mere dormitory settlements, with no lively interaction between houses but only individual connections to the outside world. Nowadays, it's possible to live more anonymously in such places than in a city. Villages like that have ceased to live. By contrast, a proper village has everything to hand and doesn't actually require a great deal from outside.

The Rechte Altstadt – that is, the part of the Old Town situated on the right (northern) bank of the River Salzach when facing downstream – is just such a village. Also known as the Andräviertel, or St Andrew's Quarter, after its main church, the district has the Linzergasse at its heart. It is small and compact, it has evolved historically and it is an entity that functions in its own right. Granted, where certain details are concerned, it is somewhat untypical. How many other villages, for example, are home to a state theatre? It's beautifully situated on the Makartplatz. And right next to it there's even a university! The Mozarteum, which has the exclusive address of Mirabellplatz 1. Founded in 1841, this educational institute for training young artists soon gained a worldwide reputation, with the name Mozart reflecting its agenda. Today, it offers students more than forty different courses. Music, drama, visual arts, composition and stage design, singing and directing, teacher training and science and, of course, tuition in numerous instruments.

Since its completion in 2006, the modern university building designed by the Munich architect Robert Rechenauer has, notwithstanding its smooth marble façade and its large expanses of plate glass, blended well into the cityscape, appearing like a gateway between the Mirabellplatz and the Makartplatz. His greatest achievement, however, is the building's interior space, with its spacious main hall, its acoustically perfect practice rooms for budding pianists, string players and flautists, and its many performance spaces where the young musicians are called upon to display their talent. Since 1998, the Mozarteum has been entitled to call itself a university. Originally founded as a music school, it is now supported by an international foundation and is also regarded as the world centre for research into Mozart.

As the music school of the 'village', therefore, it has long since outgrown its surroundings, attracting around 1,600 students from around the world. Winning a place to study here is a person's first major accolade in the realm of the arts.

It is also a very prestigious honour to hold the title of Mayor of Salzburg. For where else does a municipal leader get to reside in a Baroque palace designed by Lukas von Hildebrandt? Gerd Bacher, the legendary and longstanding director of Austrian State Radio (ORF), was an inspired and successful media figure. Yet one career goal he cherished even more than this always eluded him. He did not hanker after the federal chancellorship or the presidency of the Salzburg Festival (in time, his daughter would fill that latter position). No, what he dearly longed to be was Mayor of Salzburg.

Admittedly, one can fairly assume that it wasn't the charming Baroque *putti* which grace the marble staircase at the Mirabell Palace that drew the mover and shaker Bacher to the post, but rather the prospect of leaving his mark on the city and of bringing his seemingly inexhaustible energy to bear in rousing the place from its rustic dreaminess and narcissism. But in the event, he and Salzburg were to miss out on this experience. As an aesthete, he would surely have found nothing to object to in the mayor's office in any case, with its sweeping view over the palace gardens and the Salzach to the fortress.

A modern sensibility finds it hard to grasp that this architectural gem owes its existence to a prince-archbishop's gift to his lover. In 1606, Wolf Dietrich von Raitenau had Castle Altenau built on this spot as a residence for his lover Salome Alt and their children. Nowadays, a scandal erupts if word gets around that the village priest is in a relationship with his housekeeper. At least, such a thing was scandalous not so very long ago. Anyhow, back in those days the prince-archbishops took this location to their hearts. Wolf Dietrich's successor Markus Sittikus renamed the palace 'Mirabell' and Franz Anton, Prince of Harrach, presided over its transformation into a magnificent Baroque work of art.

And indeed, the Mirabell remains a thing of wonder to this day, as well as being a magnet for lovers. Brides and grooms from around the world plight their troth in the Marble Hall. It's thought terribly posh to do so in a place where little Wolfie Mozart once performed, with the garden as a location for wedding photos included in the price. Out there, a clearly Muslim couple are fussing about with a photographer, trying to get pictures that will be perfect mementoes of the happy day. The not exactly svelte bride is wearing a dark blue dress, with a little garland of flowers in her hair and a posy of white roses in her hand. The photographer's assistant plucks at the hem of the bride's dress. Behind, a group of girls in head-scarves stand and giggle; in our tradition, we'd call them the bridesmaids.

A little way off, an amateur violinist accompanies this scene with his rasping notes. The fellow has white hair and the tones he coaxes from his instrument have surely never been heard within the walls of the Mozarteum. Perhaps for this reason, he has shielded himself behind one of the great stone columns. The open violin case at his feet invites passers-by to make a donation.

At the far end of the garden, after passing countless groups of snapping tourists, you come across another musician, who with his accordion has long since become one of the eccentric habitués of the Mirabell. He calls himself Charlie Kamati. In fact his real, rather prosaic name is Karl Mayr, a former insurance salesman from Vöcklabruck. For more than twenty-five years he's been coming into Salzburg by train – to practise, as he puts it. On an almost daily basis now that he's a pensioner, except in winter. And he stands there at 'his pitch' at the Mirabell or, if it's raining, in pubs, and plays his instrument. Light operetta tunes, popular songs, chansons – whatever comes into his head. He thinks of himself as a clown, and on the ground to one side he's arranged some stones in the shape of a treble clef, with a little basket next to it soliciting the odd coin or two so that he can afford the next train journey from his home in Vöcklabruck into the Mecca of Music.

On the other side of Mirabell Palace, outside the main entrance, a square of the kind every town should have opens out in front of you. Every Thursday morning, from five o'clock on, it's market day here, the farmers' market. The dialect term for this in southern Germany and Austria is *die Schranne*, a word which in those regions once denoted a grain store. In Salzburg, such facilities were formerly located on Mirabell Square. Nowadays, week-in, week-out, fresh farm produce from the surrounding area is sold in front of St Andrew's Church (the Andräkirche). According to the season, this can be salad leaves, beans or strawberries. There are also stalls selling trout and lamb. And behind them, ones offering spinach and Swiss chard, all freshly picked. The place is full of noise and hubbub like any market. This colourful scene has been played out here since 1906, with just a brief break after the Second World War. The stallholders come from Salzburg, Upper Austria and Bavaria, and there's fierce competition to secure a pitch. Farmers who are interested in participating often have to wait years before they get to sell their wares here. Regionalism is the theme for this invasion of the town by the countryside. Though it's fair to say that Salzburg has never had any fear of contact with the countryside anyway. Lederhosen and *Dirndl* dresses are ubiquitous, not just at the market. Especially if you go to a performance of Hofmannsthal's *Everyman*, you'll see any number of Salzburgers in traditional garb. But that's staged in the other part of the city.

Here, on the right bank of the Salzach, you get the sense of a totally unique environment. The settlement here grew up around a bridgehead. As the connection between the two worlds, the Staatsbrücke runs directly into the Linzergasse, which forms its own little world. If you wanted to travel east – to Linz, the next largest city in Austria – you had to pass through this thoroughfare and then out through the Linzertor ('Linz Gate'). Erected in 1616, this gate protected the city from unwelcome intruders until 1894. Today the only reminders of it are the large granite slabs set in the pavement picking out the outline of the gate. Running down from here is a row of buildings with a curiously small-town infrastructure. Hardly any of the large fashion chains can be found here. They feel more at home clustered around the better known Getreidegasse. Here, rather, there is a second-hand emporium selling tin cups, CDs and books, and next door is a music shop with a range of guitars, didgeridoos and Indian sitars. In the Küchenfee ('Kitchen Fairy'), an ancient shop selling household goods, you can find preserving jars, egg slicers and trusty old lily-patterned crockery, and you can also bring your knives and scissors here to be sharpened. A combined gingerbread bakery and candle manufacturer proclaims that all its products are organic. A long-established specialist outlet for bed linen has a wrought-iron sign with gold letters hanging

from its façade, as does the 'Casanova', a nightclub, the door
to which is tucked unobtrusively inside an entranceway and
yet which still sticks out like a sore thumb in this genteel,
petit-bourgeois area. A carpet boutique, a café, a shirt shop,
a drugstore and supermarket, a chemist's, a shoe shop and a
chiropodist's – these are all strung out along the street here.
Further down, there's a grocer's selling mineral water and
Mozart-balls, with crates of fruit piled up outside the door,
full of figs, dates and grapes. Plus wild nectarines from Italy
at €2.90 for half a kilo. Pears are €4.80 per kilo. Fair enough,
the tourists will cough up those sorts of prices. Down a side
alley, you can find an electrical shop that also sells all manner
of goods, with espresso machines next to table lamps. Opposite, there's a belt maker who has his own workshop on the
first floor.

There's almost nothing that you'd need to go outside
this local, small-scale shopping environment for. And very
little here that could be accused of touristic artificiality. Of
course, the window displays are keen to include the Festival
logo and the bakery shapes pretzel dough into treble clefs to
hang in the window. But that's about the extent of it. And
wouldn't the place be swamped with foreigners in any case,
who are drawn here precisely by all this old-world charm,
including the sheer age of the buildings? One house proudly
displays the date 1475 beneath its cornice, while another is
adorned with a medallion and the year 1374. Yet many of
those who come here do so simply in order to visit a cemetery.

The small, almost square St Sebastian's cemetery, which is

situated in the middle of the Linzergasse and was founded in 1600 by Prince-Archbishop Wolf Dietrich von Raitenau, had already been a plague burial ground for a long time before that. Walking through the entrance archway with its wrought-iron gate is like journeying back in time. Gravestones and crosses are strewn about here willy-nilly over an expanse of grass. Only a handful of the graves still have a mound or even any kind of border. The cloister around the perimeter is an impressive collection of memorials to old families. But the main attraction is not the Gabriel Chapel, located in the middle of the cemetery and housing Wolf Dietrich's mausoleum, nor indeed the grave of the court master builder whom he brought in from Italy, Elia Castello, who designed the cemetery and whom fate decreed would become its first occupant after its completion. Nor is the principal attraction the family tomb of the physicist Christian Doppler or the grave of Paracelsus, whose mortal remains were only brought here in the eighteenth century and whose Latin epitaph – or at least its multilingual translation on an adjacent board – makes for general edification:

Here lies Philippus Theophrastus, Doctor of Medicine
of great renown, whose art most wonderfully healed
even the most terrible wounds, leprosy, podagra and
dropsy and other seemingly incurable diseases, and
who honoured himself by having all his possessions
distributed among the poor. He passed from life to death
on September 24 in the year 1541.

No, the main attraction, and surely the most photographed grave here, is the headstone inscribed with the name of Mozart. And this despite the fact that neither the great maestro nor his father are actually interred here in person, but only his widow Constanze and her aunt Genovefa Weber: 'Constantia von Nissen, *née* von Weber, the widow of Mozart, born at Freyberg on 6 January 1763, and died here on 6 March 1842.' This inscription and the information boards by the side of the grave mislead many tourists into thinking that this is the original Mozart family tomb. In actual fact, this monument was only put up by a Mozart admirer many years later.

As is well known, the musical genius himself is buried in Vienna, in the St Marx Cemetery. The precise spot was only identified in 1855 as being 'in all likelihood' the site of the pauper's grave where Mozart was laid to rest in 1791. Next to it, a white pillar surmounted by the figure of an angel is more of a monument than a gravestone. Visitors sometimes bridle at its rather crude design and even leave donations in the hope that the city of Vienna might honour Mozart in a more fitting way.

The place Mozart resided is far better attested than his final resting place. Admittedly, it is only one of several places where he lived and worked; in those days, moving house was like changing your shirt. Nonetheless, the musical genius stayed here in Salzburg for around eight years in an eight-room house on the Makartplatz, before moving to Vienna in 1781. The original house was destroyed during the Second

World War, but was later faithfully rebuilt and is now one of the two Mozart museums in the city, though always somewhat in the shadow of the composer's more famous birthplace in the Getreidegasse.

Although the Makartplatz can boast three truly grand civic attractions in the Mozarteum, the theatre and the Mozart Museum, it's still not *the* quintessential village square in the Rechte Altstadt. That distinction belongs to the 'Platzl', situated right at the entrance to the Old Town, immediately after the Staatsbrücke. It seems to be the fashion nowadays to have fountains springing directly out of the pavement. At three separate locations in this quarter, such water features delight children with cascades and ever-changing jets. This city has a weakness for water features. The very first of these amenities was installed at the Platzl and was clearly meant to lend the area a touch of modern urban chic, given that it's just round the corner from the Steingasse, one of the city's very oldest alleyways, which with its narrow, gloomy ambience is more of a nighttime location. Correspondingly, you'll only find small bars hereabouts, near the entrance to the Imbergstiege, a narrow flight of steps leading up to the Capuchin Monastery. A plaque on a wall in the Steingasse bears an inscription reading 'Beneath this spot lies a stone culvert, built at the behest of the following gentlemen, local house owners, in the year 1744.' It recalls the first attempt back then to tame the wild Salzach by means of a retaining stone wall.

It requires a series of such measures to turn what was formerly a village into a city suburb. Sometimes disasters take a hand in the process, like the one that occurred on the feast day of the Assumption of Mary, 15 August, in 1818. Around a hundred buildings in what was then the 'New Town' were razed to the ground by a catastrophic fire, including the chapel in the grounds of the Mirabell Palace and the Church of St Sebastian. Almost 300 families lost everything they owned. No trace of the former cityscape remained between the Linzergasse and the Mirabell Palace. Over the passage of time, the great scar left by the conflagration has healed, but for a long while after that awful night, the Bruderhof in the Linzergasse was home to a fire station and arsenal that housed six appliances. And so it comes as little surprise to find that, above the Baroque entranceway to the Mirabell Palace, a bright red banner has been hung urging people to come along to a celebration marking the 150th anniversary of the Salzburg Volunteer Fire Service. History imposes obligations.

In every small village, an invitation to a firefighters' ball at the local authority headquarters would be perfectly normal. So why shouldn't it be in Salzburg too?

9

A Picture of Salzburg

*Grey seems glaringly out of place in the
domain of Eros and colour*

EVEN ON THE EDGE OF TOWN, you can feel the pull of
the centre. Out there, where the city is largely grey and
interchangeable, any bright spots only serve to emphasise the
attractiveness of its vibrant heart. The transition between city
and country is rarely pretty anywhere. But in a city with an
aesthetically beautiful centre, the mixture of ugliness and
arbitrary development that characterises its outskirts is even
more glaringly obvious than elsewhere.

As in other cities, the fringes of Salzburg are also hall-
marked by rows of low-rise housing from former eras punctu-
ated by huge barns of buildings. Car showrooms with acres of
plate-glass and concrete, warehouses painted in bold colours
as dictated by the company's design ethos, commercial enter-
prises, supermarkets, petrol stations and shopping malls. The
region surrounding Salzburg has only a handful of major
industrial plants. The city has been a centre of commerce

since time immemorial. In a place where high mountains afford a fine view into the wide blue yonder, both ideas and trade can develop more freely. The intersection here with the region of Bavaria proved to be the gateway to the prosperous West. At a time when Austria was not yet a member of the European Union and border posts with toll barriers were still in place up on the Walserberg, Salzburg was the first stop-off point for imports. Even today, some Austrian head offices of large German firms are still to be found in Salzburg, while the glass temples of the automotive trade are just markers of small-town mediocrity.

And in the midst of all this, like a great poster, stands a painting of Salzburg. It jostles for attention among billboards advertising toothpaste, furniture and hamburgers, yet still manages to stand out. Between bold splashes of colour suggesting brushstrokes stands an image of the fortress in the city centre. The foreground is dominated by bright sunny yellows and fresh greens, while the garden of the Mirabell is shown in all its blooming summer pomp. Off to one side, the cathedral, the Franciscan Church and the Collegiate Church are sketched in. And presiding over this scene is a bright blue expanse of sky, broken only by the odd cloud. In other words, it's an ideal picture of Salzburg. A picture-postcard scene with an artistic twist. No matter whether they are approaching from the north or the west, new arrivals driving into the city are greeted by this idyllic image sited at the entrance to an underground car park in the suburb of Aigen, immediately after the airport exit.

This, then, is how Salzburg wants to be seen. Underneath the picture are banners promoting the next major upcoming event in the city: Harvest Festival, the Advent Market, Mozart Week or the St Rupert's Day Fair (Rupertikirtag). For the past two decades, this greeting has been displayed at all the main entry points to the city; its popularity rests on the fact that the local news bulletin of the national broadcast network ORF also used this same image as a backdrop for five years, from 1997 to 2002.

This raises the question as to whether the creator of the painting still stands by this idyllic picture of Salzburg nowadays. To find out, you need to leave the city. To the northeast, a short stretch on the motorway, out onto the plain. The area round here is called the Flachgau – which literally means 'flat region' – though 'flat' is a relative term. The landscape here consists of rolling hills covered with lush pastures, little patches of woodland, neat villages, and several lakes for recreational activities. As it's in the catchment area of the state capital, there's a lot of traffic on the roads.

After about 25 kilometres, you reach Neumarkt am Wallersee, where everyone knows the studio of Hans Weyringer. Little wonder, as the house is far from being your customary charming, hard-to-find artist's studio; instead, it has a wide frontage with marble sculptures outside and, next to it, an open-air, roofed compound housing a number of large tree trunks, some of them as yet unworked, while others already show clear sculptural contours. Behind the studio there is a large garden that has been turned into a sculpture park containing finished works in marble, granite, serpentine, glass or wood.

A collection of huge stone rollers lies off to one side; made from finely polished granite, they are so-called 'centre rolls' originally used in paper mills. These monsters are perfect cylinders, each weighing several tons, that have now been retired from service. Weyringer has acquired them from all over Europe and plans to use them to create a sculpture avenue by planting them upright in the ground and placing his sculptures on top like capitals. One such pillar has already been erected.

The studio itself consists of two cavernous workshops with a library in between. One of the workspaces, which has a crane on a gantry in the ceiling space, is for heavy wood sculptures. Hanging all along the wall, like exhibits in a museum, are handsaws, old wood planes in every conceivable width, and hammers and crowbars, arranged according to weight. Next to these are chainsaws of various sizes, similarly spick and span, lined up in serried ranks. Various maquettes for larger sculptures, made from fine marble or metal, give an indication of future projects. There's no hint here of the creative chaos that some artists apparently need to surround themselves with, nor is there any sign of offcuts or other debris strewn about. It's a practice he learnt in his father's carpentry workshop. He regards cleanliness and tidiness as the basic prerequisites for working.

In the other workroom, his painter's studio, stacks of pictures sit piled up against the walls, with a few also on easels.

Some of them are finished, others barely started. Paint tubes, pestles and paintbrushes are once again neatly arranged. The wide glass frontage of the building looks out over the sculpture garden and the gentle landscape beyond, and in front of the windows, to one side stands ... a bathtub. A jacuzzi, just plonked down there. Not so that the artist can take a dip when he feels like it, but rather as a symbol of his sense of cleanliness. It has been painted, in typical Weyringer style, with bold brushstrokes in primary colours. There's no place for sombreness here. This is the home of colour and of Eros. One recurring motif is large-breasted angels, also in the form of frescoes. On a board, there's a figure in clay, possibly still a study, the preparatory work for a bronze casting. It depicts a reclining woman, naked and with her legs splayed. In the adjoining room there is a series of paintings showing Aphrodite in various poses, but never bashful. None of the women on his canvases ever have a stitch of clothing on. They're always naked and invitingly displaying the centre of their womanhood.

In the background are some colourful landscapes, depicting the summer in full vigour. And hanging on the wall there's also a cityscape of Salzburg in the winter.

Over a bottle of good Riesling, Weyringer recounts the story of his large, famous summer view of Salzburg. Painted in 1996, it formed the centrepiece of a series featuring all the regions of the federal state of Salzburg. Since then, the original of this specially commissioned work, which measures 146 by 346 centimetres, has hung in the headquarters of the energy company Salzburg AG, an imposing complex of buildings designed by Wilhelm Holzbauer. Weyringer painted the scene from the mayor's office in Mirabell Palace. He was permitted to work there for several days while the mayor Josef Dechant was away on his travels and he could get an unimpeded view over the gardens to the fortress. Weyringer always paints from nature in situ. On the initiative of various media companies, he gave permission for the image to be reproduced on large-size posters at the main entry points to the city, where they remain to this day.

But does that picture still reflect the image he has of Salzburg? 'Sure, although –' he begins, but then digresses to talk about his background and career. His father had a carpentry business, where he learned the trade and took his master craftsman's exam before moving to Vienna to study architecture under Friedrich Janeba and Roland Rainer. But although this allowed him to add the letters 'M.Arch' to his business card, he never wanted to work as an architect. And so he became an artist. In this role, he actually styles himself 'Johann Weyringer' in order to distinguish himself from his father, who is also called Hans. But everyone still knows him as Hans as well. So when the artist Johann talks about Salzburg, it is both with the background of a formal training in architecture and town planning and with the no-nonsense attitude of the carpenter Hans. Accordingly, his views on the subject are both lucid and down-to-earth.

He likes the city but not its outskirts. 'The roads into the city are lined with horrible, run-down detached houses and cheap apartment blocks,' he says with visible irritation, 'but the politicians don't seem capable of doing anything to change that.' The architectural gem that is Salzburg is confined to the city of the prince-archbishops. What angers him above all about the 'horrors' beyond this small central zone is the fact that it could all be so very different. But when anyone tries to do anything about it, you can bet your bottom dollar there's always someone there to scupper it. An idiotic wrangling designed to frustrate change is what Weyringer calls it, a petty mindset. He just doesn't get it.

His criticism is also aimed at the greater Salzburg region, from Golling in the Tennengau district to Straßwalchen in the Flachgau, where a densely populated strip of housing is taking shape, a built-up conurbation the size of a town. Weyringer regards this as an example of haphazard piecemeal development, where the proper planning of land use often goes by the board and with vital infrastructure projects constantly being blocked by opposition. The painter sees this as a sell-out and as a policy of obstruction for obstruction's sake. 'The Greens get up in arms and talk down every proposal just in order to parade their environmental credentials,' he says, pulling no punches. 'It's a miracle how Mayor Heinz Schaden puts up with it all. He's still trying to build consensus across party lines,' Weyringer notes approvingly, but if it weren't for that, political small-mindedness would inevitably make problems far greater than they need be, he claims.

Weyringer has visited and painted many cities, including Moscow, London and Paris. 'If you're in a place for any length of time, then ultimately any city becomes a small town, a provincial backwater, probably even New York,' the Salzburg artist muses; what he's driving at here is that, as just an occasional visitor to a city, you can never appreciate all its problems.

The centre of Salzburg has even improved, he claims, in spite of the fact that the Getreidegasse is now populated by identical shops, just like in every other city, be it Berlin or Venice. 'The tourist tat from China that they sell is the same wherever you go, but at least Salzburg is growing. Venice is shrinking, with people moving out of the city.' When he was a kid, he recalls, they'd go into the old city centre to do their shopping, because there were still independent shops there in those days, like Eisensteiner's in the Judengasse, or Roither's or Flatscher's in the Getreidegasse. Or Schauer the butcher's in the Steingasse, or Seppele's the secondhand shop in the Linzergasse, or the Platzlkeller on the Platzl. 'The department store chains nowadays have a global feel to them – but for all that, Salzburg's still a village,' is his clear verdict. 'And a wonderful village at that,' he adds.

One thing is a source of sheer delight for him: 'For at least five weeks in the summer, Salzburg's got a real metropolitan feel to it, otherwise it's a little town trapped between the local mountain ranges. But the city benefits from its position close to the Alps, which makes for some marvellous contrasts,' he announces, reverting to full painterly mode. And he proceeds to enthuse about moods, sight lines and colours. He says he could sell pictures of Salzburg 'by the shedload', but he only embarks on one if he can find a new angle to exploit. A new vista or a different way of looking at the townscape; it can take a long time for such an image to mature in his head.

The sheer beauty of the city, its aura and its equilibrium, has him in raptures. The Baroque period, its golden age, really speaks to him. Even so, he only finds Salzburg a city of the arts to a limited degree, since music eclipses everything else here. That much is abundantly clear at the Mozarteum, the painter claims, and becomes agitated once more: 'Where practitioners of fine art are concerned, the Mozarteum isn't a proper art academy at all, at best just a university for handicrafts. The teaching staff there are stuffed shirts, not creative artists, but they still manage to get themselves onto all the prize juries, where they spout crap,' he froths. His diatribe is aimed chiefly at female art administrators, whom he calls 'cultural apparatchiks'. Having got this off his chest, he takes a gulp of Riesling and a bite of the South Tyrolean *saucisson sec* that his friend Sepp Forcher has brought along for him.

So, does he still regard himself as a Salzburger? 'Yes and no.' His first exhibitions were staged there: at the Georg-Trakl-House, the Galerie Welz and the Residenzgalerie. At that time, he got to know the city well, though he never felt emotionally rooted in it. He comes from Sighartstein near Neumarkt and was born Johann Karl Strickner, because his parents only got married subsequently. His forebears had migrated there from the area around the Brenner Pass. His great uncle Karl Weyringer had made a name for himself in Vienna as a seed merchant and 'recreational and ornamental gardener', as they were called back then. The Weyringergasse in the 4th District of Vienna is named after him. Maybe there'll be a Weyringergasse in Salzburg one day too. Hans has already been awarded the City Seal in silver, and his public art is present in many city squares, with seven of his sculptures at the Technology Centre alone, plus a 7-metre-high work in steel, stained glass and gold leaf outside the airport. Admittedly, this latter work is not without its critics in the city. Indeed, generally speaking Hans the sculptor is much more controversial a figure than Hans the painter.

He's a good communicator. Others see him as being very business savvy. In any event, up until now he has only trusted himself to market his own work. But if he's planning on conquering the international art market, he couldn't avoid engaging the services of a major gallery owner.

He is obsessed with work. He has already created almost 6,000 paintings. When he was younger he was a keen glider pilot and mountaineer but now, aside from his family, there's only art. Sculpture takes the most time and effort. His work *Magic Flute Stone* involved more than 2,000 hours' labour. And the materials he used cost some 40,000 euros besides. He'd just sold this colossus, made from serpentine from East Tyrol and weighing in at 14 metric tons, to a private buyer in Salzburg, who built the entrance hall to his house around the piece.

And he is also a religious person. His mother was deeply devout, and his brother and one of his nephews are priests. For many decades, Rome has been a really important place for him and he's currently working on two 8-metre-high glass panels for the internal entrance wall in the church of Santa Maria dell'Anima, with its seminary for trainee priests from German-speaking countries. In 2013, he completed his most spectacular commission to date for the sacristy there: a portrait of Pope Benedict XVI. The Salzburg artist created this as a double portrait in glass, involving a screen-printed photo of the pontiff in office, set amidst several boldly coloured planes, next to a portrait of Benedict seated, a more personal take on the Pope by Weyringer.

Pope Benedict granted the artist an audience of 50 minutes to make the preliminary sketches for this work, though originally just quarter of an hour had been set aside for this. The two men spoke about art and religion, with the former pontiff – who hails from Germany – sitting on a white couch in a white cassock and wearing white socks with brown leather sandals. Opposite him sat the artist, dressed soberly and respectfully in a dark blue suit. A bandaged finger on Weyringer's right hand did not hinder the ambidextrous artist in the slightest in sketching away diligently. He knelt down to work, as the little table in front of him was so low to the ground and also because of the perspective. 'Normally I kneel before Almighty God, and now I'm kneeling before the Pope,' he quipped as an opening gambit, and went on to have a very enjoyable conversation with the old man. Some years had passed since then, but he still speaks enthusiastically about how he'd never met such a clever person before. Although it hadn't been the Pope's decision that Weyringer should paint his portrait, he was perfectly amenable to the idea. He knew all his previous works, the artist recounted, including the very revealing nudes. Now a large photo of this meeting hangs in the studio at Neumarkt, between the nudes.

He ascribes the fact that he was permitted to sit opposite the Pope and sketch him to his obsession with the principle of only ever painting from nature. If he needs elephants as his models, he flies to Namibia. He has also set up his easel on the Himalayas and on the slopes of Mount Kilimanjaro before now. And of course in the mayor's office in Mirabell Palace, from where he captured the beautiful old Salzburg of the prince-archbishops.

The image of the other part of the city, the much larger part beyond the centre, doesn't interest him as an artist.

10

Art in Search of Buyers

Klimt, Kubin and Kokoschka – but no price tags, please!

THIS GALLERY DOESN'T simply have a doorway, it has an entrance portal. And it's closed. Above it stands a coat of arms: an imperial double-headed eagle beneath a crown on the left, and to the right a hand reaching for a cross. These point to the history of the building, not its current usage. For that, you need to glance up and to one side, at the building's façade. There's a bronze figure dangling there, a man in a squatting pose, with his hands pressed flat to the ground beside his feet, as though he were about to catapult himself out horizontally from the wall. This athletic figure is the work of British sculptor Antony Gormley. On top of the portal is a balustrade from which a banner has been hung with the legend 'Elger Esser' in large letters, the name of a German photographic artist. An elegant sign next to the door reads 'Galerie Ropac'. Underneath are the opening times and the instruction 'Please ring the bell'.

So that's what I do. In response, an electronic buzz grants

me access through one wing of the heavy wooden doors. A young woman sitting at reception explains in a friendly and efficient manner what pieces the gallery currently has on show. Her name is Susanne; she's the gallery's digital manager and loves her beautiful place of work. Small wonder in such a house of international repute. Her gaze comes to rest on imposing, exclusive works of art, unaffordable for her and for most of the gallery's visitors, but nonetheless these constitute her daily surroundings.

It's likely you'll find yourself all alone as you wander through the rooms. That figures – the festival period is over. Salzburg is thronged with visitors, but they're all city sightseers, not art buyers. So you have the place to yourself. The larger rooms are occupied almost exclusively by large-format paintings. There aren't many of them, but they are all the more imposing for that. At first glance, Elger Esser's photographic works, prints on Alu-Dibond measuring 2 metres and more across, are not even identifiable as such. The dense tangle of plants they depict, which draws the viewer's eye into the image, looks like it was painted. Thistles, thyme and mysterious shadows of plants. Next to these are some appreciably smaller pictures showing dazzling sunsets. Printed on silvered copper plates, they tell a story of the radiance of the world and its decline. The first floor of the gallery is devoted to modern art classics. Anselm Kiefer, a mixed-media artist who both paints and sculpts, is represented by one enormous work. A mountain rendered in various shades of grey, possibly with snowfields up near the summit, while at the bottom of the picture the behemoth is reflected in a body of water. In front of the painting hangs a metal funnel, positioned as though it were trying to suck the dense corporeality of the painting into itself. Beside this, the work of Alex Katz appears all the more colourful. Faces in clear, smooth planes of colour, bonhomie with a rear exit. And on the floor there is a large white sculpture by Erwin Wurm. More sculptural pieces can be found in the garden, at the rear of which you get a view over the grounds of Mirabell Palace and the fortress. The villa couldn't be more beautifully positioned.

A side wing calls itself the 'drawing cabinet', no doubt solely because the rooms here have lower ceilings, though they're no less impressively stocked. They are full of graphic works by Georg Baselitz. You enter the cabinet through a heavy black steel door that is fitted with an encoded lock and surveillance camera for added security, and which is opened remotely from the reception desk. Once you're inside, electrically operated bolts slide back into place. You feel imprisoned, like in a bank vault. Alone again. None of the pictures carry a price tag. After you've taken everything in, the vault door can be opened unexpectedly easily from the inside, and you find yourself back in the world of the profane once more.

It's not particularly large, this gallery, with just a ground and first floor and a frontage that is only five windows wide. But it is very prestigious. And still considerably larger than the premises in the Kaigasse where Thaddaeus Ropac began to ply his trade as a gallery owner in 1983. When Andy Warhol first set foot in this mini-gallery the following year, he clutched his head in horror at the thought of who he might have got himself involved with. However, horror soon gave way to an amicable enthusiasm. Today Ropac is one of the big players in the world's fine art market.

In 1990, soon after relocating to Villa Kast – this Art Nouveau building abutting the Mirabell Palace gardens, which even today still bears the name of its former owners, the aristocratic Kast von Ebelsberg family – he opened his first gallery in the Marais quarter of Paris, a premises with 1,000 square metres of floor space. In 2010, the business expanded in Salzburg with the acquisition of a 2,500-square-metre former industrial building just outside the Old Town, which has since been rechristened simply 'The Salzburg Hall'. Expansion on the Seine followed in 2012 to a former metal goods factory in the northeast of the city, not far from the new Philharmonie de Paris. The gallery there covers more than 5,000 square metres. There's many a museum that would be delighted to fill that much exhibition space. Ropac has no trouble keeping it well stocked. What's more, he's since expanded still further, opening his fifth gallery in London's Mayfair in 2017.

He started out as an outsider who couldn't even afford proper frames for the pictures he bought. He had actually wanted to become an artist himself. At the time, the summer academy founded at Hohensalzburg Fortress by the painter Oskar Kokoschka had captured his imagination. He was up there every day, imbibing the spirit of Kokoschka, who in fact was no longer alive by then, but who was still the great guiding inspiration behind many of the major figures of the art scene. Ropac laid the groundwork for his later enterprise by fostering contacts with young artists from Austria, Germany and Italy. He then went on to become Joseph Beuys's assistant. Beuys too was rather sniffy about Ropac's first faltering steps as a gallery owner in Salzburg, but this connection proved key to establishing relationships with artists like Keith Haring, Andy Warhol and Roy Lichtenstein. After they died, the prices of their works skyrocketed – and Ropac also profited.

From his little showroom in the Kaigasse in Salzburg, he set about generating his own market. 'You can create markets, and of course at that time in Salzburg there simply wasn't one,' Ropac candidly explains. Today, his gallery is a 'Who's Who' of the fine art world – the British artist Tony Cragg, the German Daniel Richter, the Austrian Arnulf Rainer, the Swiss resident Georg Baselitz and the New Yorker Alex Katz. Those on the scene who command the highest prices, in other words.

There's no question that Paris has more market potential than little Salzburg. The Salzburg Festival acts as a catalyst, a showcase for art lovers, but the customer base here isn't nearly broad enough for the global market, Ropac says, recalling his early years: 'Back then, I'd underestimated the fact that the festival atmosphere is limited to just a few weeks a year, in summer, and then at Easter. Outside of those times Salzburg lapses back into a kind of numb torpor that can really be quite disconcerting.'

The famous gallery owner, with his gently wavy hair and his distinctive spectacles, is of one mind on this matter with his local competitors. As far as they're concerned, he's not a rival but rather a magnet who attracts cash-rich punters to the banks of the Salzach. And because not everyone can afford a Baselitz or a Kiefer, there's plenty of business to go round the other galleries.

All told, there are well over a dozen of them in the city. Though according to Siegfried Karrer, founder of Galerie Weihergut in the Linzergasse, not all of them can really be counted as galleries in the classic sense. 'Lots of them like to style themselves as that, though in actual fact they're just art dealers.' A true gallery owner's business is to search out new talent and find a public for it, whereas all an art dealer does is market artists who have already been discovered. '"Art dealer" is pretty much a term of abuse in the mouths of gallery owners,' says Karrer.

The Palais Kuenberg in the Sigmund-Haffner-Gasse – right in the heart of the city, just a stone's throw away from the Festival Hall and the cathedral square – is home to the oldest of the classic galleries of Salzburg. This gallery is nothing short of a role model for Karrer. After all, it nurtured classic Austrian Modernism throughout its heyday, well into the second half of the twentieth century. In 1909, the place had been a shop selling picture frames, which Friedrich Welz, the son of the firm's founder, then turned into a gallery. It held its first exhibitions in the 1930s. Nowadays Galerie Welz is owned by a consortium of partners, one of whom is its managing director, Hubert Lendl. His office is accessed by climbing a staircase from the neat and well-organised show-room on the ground floor and passing through a series of rooms containing ever more densely stacked piles of pictures.

A state of uproar, the MD calls it, though he has a clear oversight of all the holdings in his head. The gallery manages artists often over a period of many years, and exhibitions are happening non-stop – which all adds up to a lot of artworks. The gallery has its own publishing arm which is responsible for producing all the relevant publications. Lendl lives sur-rounded by pictures at home too, but at least they remain in his possession. In the gallery, he is sometimes loath to part with certain paintings that he has grown fond of. Which is something that artists themselves often experience. But busi-ness is business. And business is booming. Especially the trade in big-name artists.

The gallery became a major player by selling the works of Kokoschka, Klimt and Kubin. Along with those of sculptors like Alfred Hrdlicka, Josef Pillhofer or Herbert Albrecht. 'The successors to Wotruba,' as Lendl calls that group. Fritz Wotruba himself was also shown here from very early on in his career.

Contemporary art finds a place here too. Mind you, the gallery is pretty choosy; you won't find anything crazily avant-garde or any really young artists on show. Nor do Salzburg artists have it any easier, either. The gallery doesn't want to be too local. An artist's work needs to be properly established before it gains entry. Accordingly, the gallery's catchment area extends from Vienna to Munich. Galerie Welz is happy to leave newcomers to the other galleries. Indeed, generally speaking, a fiercely competitive relationship doesn't appear to exist among the many galleries. Each of them does its own thing.

Galerie Mauroner on the Residenzplatz exhibits primarily Spanish art, plus some Italian and French, but also the work of out-and-out mavericks such as Jan Fabre or Madeleine Berkhemer. Mario Mauroner has the luxury here of juggling between his two sites in Vienna and Salzburg. The gallery began in 1972 as a student gallery called 'Academia'. In the meantime, several other galleries dealing in the work of young artists have also emerged, such as Galerie Trapp in the Griesgasse. The gallery at the Georg-Trakl-House on Waag-platz, which is owned by the province of Salzburg, is quite unequivocally devoted to promoting young artistic talent. In addition to an open studio there, there is also a professional workshop producing graphic prints, where up to forty artists work over the course of a year. The museum retains a copy of every work printed there.

Current contact with the summer academy is maintained above all by the Salzburg House of Artists (Künstlerhaus). Galerie Welz also had a historical connection to the academy up at the fortress. In the 1950s, Friedrich Welz was the driving force behind and the organiser of the 'School of Seeing' founded by Oskar Kokoschka. But history is a sensitive area where this gallery is concerned. During the National Socialist period, Welz was one of the foremost art dealers of the Third

Reich. This brilliant man was truly adept at playing the Nazi system. As an early member of the NSDAP, he bought and sold artworks for all he was worth, showing no qualms about dealing in Aryanised art yet at the same time not shying away from trading in works that the Nazis had declared 'degenerate'. He bought and squirrelled away a lot of pictures; the regime knew full well what this colourful character was up to, but turned a blind eye. That became valuable capital after the National Socialist period. In the same way that he had previously styled himself as a Nazi, so he now presented himself as their sworn enemy. Deploying all his considerable charm and energy, he continued to thrive and to foster close contacts with the political elite. Official honours and distinctions followed and, on the founding of the 'Rupertinum Gallery of Modern Art and Graphic Collection' in 1977, he was appointed its first rector. He had finally achieved his goal of having founded not only a gallery but also a museum (or at least co-founded it in the case of the latter).

To date, no one has ever fully investigated the story of his activities. Siegfried Karrer suspects that Galerie Welz and the Residenzgalerie may yet have to deal with a number of restitution cases. No one's bringing any pressure to bear right now, though. Even for Hubert Lendl, there are still several unresolved questions relating to the gallery's founder, who during his lifetime accorded little importance to keeping traceable records of his dealings. But this no longer impinges on the gallery's current business. Lendl devotes all his efforts to organising, year-in year-out, nine major exhibitions, invariably including one with an international focus around the time of the Festival. Works by Chagall, Miró and Picasso have already been shown at this event, as well as Emil Schumacher, Josef Mikl, Markus Prachensky and Wolfgang Hollegha. Well-known names, in other words. Also, by exhibiting works by German Expressionists, the gallery is consciously appealing to visitors from Austria's northern neighbour, though Emil Nolde and Lyonel Feininger don't just sell to Germans. Some of their works even stay in Austria, Lendl is pleased to report.

But however important the Festival period might be in general, it's not the be-all and end-all for the fine art sector. Karrer explains that Galerie Weihergut recently recorded better sales figures in September than during the Festival period. These sales included a number of extremely expensive pictures, mainly to Salzburgers who had decamped from the city in August. Generally speaking, Salzburg only accounts for 30 per cent of his annual turnover, a good third of it during the Festival period. Easter is no longer as significant. 'When Karajan was here, he attracted a really refined and artistically knowledgeable audience. But that's all over now.' So Karrer now does the lion's share of his business at trade fairs, and travels extensively to Paris and Los Angeles.

He couldn't live from sales in Salzburg alone, and this has given him a very dim view of his home market. 'Salzburgers aren't as affected by the art bug as is often claimed. A couple of times a year they have a little fling with art, but apart from that everything that's on offer here is imported.'

Salzburg is still at its most authentic in its music, he maintains. A clear imbalance exists between music and the visual
arts, where, he claims, there is a lack of development work and
support for the local scene. Of course, one area unaffected by
all this is amateur painting, which greatly impairs the market
potential of serious home-grown art – so says the man who
himself paints for recreation and who, through the painting
seminars he holds, has done much to cultivate his own competition. 'For the most part, it's lady artists; their works sell
like hot cakes and flood the market. But they're just decoration, not art.' No gallery takes their stuff, but there's many a
framing business whose turnover is made up almost entirely
of amateur art.

So, gallery owner Siegfried Karrer has his concerns about
the market, though for a long time his greatest worry was
about his business. Although he wanted to stop and play a
behind-the-scenes role organising exhibitions, he couldn't
find a successor. His son was already active in the international art world and had no interest in the gallery in the
Linzergasse in Salzburg. And so his father came to realise
that it can be more difficult closing a gallery than opening
one. Until, that is, a former colleague finally plucked up
the courage to take the plunge into the uncertain waters of
gallery ownership and took over the business.

So it was that fate came to his aid by bowling him a curve
ball, just like it did at the outset. Karrer was a manager at
an international oil company. Before that, this native Salzburger had studied engineering and learned the violin at the

Mozarteum. He would have loved to become a conductor, but the world of commerce won out. Until, that is, he was involved in a serious car crash and barely escaped with his life. That was the signal that he should change career. So he started managing an artist, got to know the art scene and founded his gallery. To this day, he retains a connection with music by doing some composing and through collecting rare and valuable violins. This is Salzburg, after all. But the visual arts became a genuine passion for him, in particular the urge to enthuse other people about art. What he enjoys most is hearing children jabbering away about what they see in a painting. He also breaks down adults' fears of the mysteries of art by patiently explaining, for example, what the numbers in front of and after a diagonal line at the bottom of prints mean.

Most likely he'll have to end up selling his enormous stock – literally thousands of pictures in two full warehouses – piecemeal to other gallery owners. However, the sector is very cautious as the market is saturated right now. And anyhow, hardly anyone is brave enough to start branching out in new directions – so much is clear from the holdings of museums, where it's mostly familiar names that are exhibited. And in any case, international rather than local artists. Museums acquire everything they want, including even the most expensive pieces, just as long as they're able to pay the insurance premiums, an insider explains. For nowadays, that's an expense artists can save themselves if they don't have to stockpile works in their own studios. Plus it helps raise their market value.

And so the same rubric holds good throughout. Artists and works that are well known have pulling power, attracting the public to museums and assuring the galleries healthy profits. Admittedly, often it's not the art that's being sold but the name. This is art as stocks and shares.

Yet the really blue-chip stock – artworks with very prestigious signatures, that is – aren't the norm for Salzburg galleries. Though some sculptures have been sold for several hundreds of thousands of euros, Hubert Lendl reveals. Such as those created by the big names of the international scene, provided they can be acquired for showing.

Generally speaking, this matter of prices is a controversial business. In their displays, the gallery owners are very discreet, not giving any indication of the price for the most part. Or, as in Galerie Welz, they make do with codes. A bronze sculpture by Herbert Albrecht has a tag bearing the price code 'kt'. Or on the first floor, near the stairs, there's an inconspicuous picture, measuring just 12 by 15 centimetres, comprising a piece of simple corrugated cardboard with a hole in it and an ink sketch on it. But the work is by Antoni Tàpies, the Spanish Surrealist and Dadaist who died in 2012. Underneath it is the code 'nu'. 'Anyone who didn't know what the score was here would be flabbergasted if they saw €30,000 on the ticket. That is why we prefer using letters,' Lendl explains. Thus, 'nu' signifies 30,000 euros.

Galerie Ropac has no need for that kind of thing. You'll search in vain there for price lists or any indication whatsoever of cost. Whenever an exhibition is held here – and

Ropac and his eighty members of staff in Paris and Salzburg organise around thirty each year – a lot of the exhibits have been sold in advance. If a gallery wants to show the work of an artist of international standing, it is obliged to pre-purchase around a quarter of the works that are sent for exhibiting. Otherwise it's a non-starter. Normal galleries simply don't have that kind of clout.

As a result, middle-ranking galleries have to bank on works that people in Austria know and can afford. Their target group is the solid middle class, who want to buy status symbols that friends and neighbours will recognise as such.

Art speculation and artificially generated hype about particular artists are not unknown among the large gallery groups, but these astronomical prices right at the top of the market are another world entirely, and do run the risk that a bubble will suddenly burst. The Salzburg galleries can't compete in that game; the works they have for sale usually have prices that can easily be compared on the market. The only Salzburg gallery owner who moves in the upper spheres is Thaddaeus Ropac.

His colleagues in Salzburg hold him in high esteem, no doubt also because his success has had such a powerful knock-on effect on the whole gallery scene in the city of Mozart. Certainly in the summer, when the city as a whole likes to think of itself as a Mecca for the arts.

11

Whodunnits for Everyman

Murder and manslaughter in the most
beautiful setting ever for skulduggery

DEATH IS UGLY. Certainly the fact of death is ugly, and
all the more so when it involves a corpse on public view.
In the heart of the city, right in front of the cathedral, what's
more. A dead body is discovered lying prone on the *Every-*
man stage on the cathedral square; it's shoeless, and sticking
out of its chest is a cheap replica of a Renaissance dagger.

So, a clear instance of murder. Such events always deeply
unsettle the neighbourhood, the deceased's relatives and the
city in general. And in this case the world of the Salzburg
Festival too. After all, the dead body in question is Death.
Well, not literally, but rather the person playing Death. An
actor, in other words, the one who has had to portray Death
on stage any number of times, has now abruptly and involun-
tarily come face-to-face with his character. Life really can be
that ugly, at least in a novel.

From the very beginning, its author took a gamble with

this spectacular piece of villainy. Manfred Baumann was quite rational in calculating the likely success of his chosen plot. He wanted to come up with a sensational case, and what could possibly raise more eyebrows in Salzburg than a murder bang in front of the hallowed cathedral, at festival time, with the maximum number of people in the city and any number of glamorous celebrities flitting about, who instantly find themselves conveniently added to the long list of suspects? Bumping off the actor who plays Everyman struck him as a bit too obvious, and so it was that Death had to bite the dust. The title of the novel, *Jedermanntod (Everyman Death)* even managed to combine the two characters.

His plan paid off; a publisher was found, and Baumann's debut novel duly appeared in 2010, to great acclaim. Since then, the author has turned it into a series, with his main character, Commissar Merana, dashing from case to case. So far, Baumann has rattled off no fewer than six Salzburg crime thrillers from his keyboard. Merana becomes ever more slick in his crime-solving, in a way that his real-life counterparts never could. At the time of *Everyman Death*, the commissar is forty-three years old and clearly has a great deal of experience in investigating violent crimes. But how much experience in solving murder cases could one really gain in Salzburg?

Basically, none. The crime statistics show that in recent times, an average of precisely one murder per year has taken place in Salzburg. In addition, there have been a few attempted murders: four in 2014, two in 2013 and as many as seven in 2012. In 2015 an altercation between two young men had a fatal outcome. The city police proudly report that every single one of these crimes has been cleared up. That could actually come from the pages of a crime novel, given that cases are always successfully solved in them too. Salzburg is a really peaceful place, then, as is the surrounding region; a handful of similar crimes over the same period occurred there as well, but the sum total hardly makes for the long run of experience a detective might expect to amass in solving spectacular cases. Perhaps, though, the sheer rarity of a genuine murder case in Salzburg spurs the police on to make a special effort, which in turn produces a clear-up rate of 100 per cent.

Besides, there are countless examples of whodunnits whose success does not depend upon reflecting unvarnished reality. All the reader is required to do is to imagine that such-and-such a thing could happen, or could have happened. But that's a difficult enough trick for an author. Even when policemen write novels, such as the Salzburg CID officer Oskar Feifar whose crime thrillers are set in Lower Austria, the fictional detectives they feature have immeasurably more experience in solving cases than they could ever acquire in real life.

But in any case, in his novels, Manfred Baumann does not make the commissar a hero who outshines everyone else, but instead places the city centre stage. When he devises a story, he starts by determining the setting.

Choosing the *Everyman* stage as the scene of the crime was a deliberate ploy. There's scarcely any character so popular in Salzburg as Everyman. Provided they inhabit the role at all successfully, the various actors who play him attain unimagined levels of popularity. The performers weren't always as popular as they have become in recent years. Whenever Peter Simonischek, during his eight seasons playing Everyman, used to walk around the city, he drew people's gazes and captured their hearts just like that. And hardly anything changed when he handed over to Nicholas Ofczarek. From 2013 to 2016, Cornelius Obonya played the role. Before the performance, when the whole cast of actors and musicians used to walk in procession from the Festival Hall across the Alter Markt to the cathedral square, that was a spectacle in itself even for those who didn't have a ticket. For the Everyman actor, each new parade was a triumphal march. In passing, Obonya would shake as many hands as a politician on the election stump. Of course, coming as he does from the great Austrian Hörbiger thespian dynasty, Obonya is a star. But over the years of their reign, every actor who plays Everyman becomes the carnival prince of Salzburg. They already need to be established stars in order to secure this role. Yet when Obonya's successor Tobias Moretti found himself temporarily indisposed through illness in 2018, and the young actor Philipp Hochmair had to step in once or twice at short notice, the latter was fêted for his bravura performance as if the old Everyman legends Alexander Moissi or Attila Hörbiger had risen from the grave.

The Everyman launch party is always a hugely well-attended society event. It was once held at the Krimpelstätter beer cellar and restaurant but has latterly taken place at the Stieglkeller. Astonishingly, the question of who will play the

Buhlschaft ('Paramour'), the most sought-after supporting role in the acting world, and even more crucially what dress she will wear, has taken something of a back seat in recent times – and this despite the fact that the Residenzgalerie staged an exhibition of the various dresses worn by this character over the years.

Every year without fail, even if the greatest opera stars are due to perform, no production at the Salzburg Festival is such a sure-fire sell-out as *Everyman*. Some people claim to have tried unsuccessfully for years before finally obtaining tickets.

The absolute highest accolade for a member of the *Everyman* fan community is to be inducted into the circle of 'Everyman Callers'. Your voice needs to register at least 100 decibels, and amplifiers are shunned. And it takes about 120 decibels for the caller who is positioned up on the ramparts of the fortress to be heard clearly down on the square as he reminds his victim Everyman of his impending death. The other three callers are up in the towers of the churches of St Francis and St Peter and in the cathedral cloisters. In the past some directors have altered their number and positions and kept this secret beforehand so as to have the maximum impact on the audience. Each booming 'Jeeeedeeermaaaaann!' call must be delivered crisply, at different voice pitches and in a single breath, and with no hint of yelling, so that it strikes terror into the listeners. Normally the callers are an officially confirmed team; on just one occasion has a 'guest star' been allowed to take part – but naturally only after a thorough vocal examination by the ensemble doctor. The current

principal caller, the surgeon Boris Todoroff, who is now resident in Vienna, has seen the death of every Everyman since he
was a boy – Walter Reyer, Curd Jürgens, Maximilian Schell,
Klaus Maria Brandauer and all the rest. In 2014, he had the
honour of summoning Cornelius Obonya to meet his fate.
'As the chief caller I was behind the stage, and I called twice,
and then each of the echoing callers in the church towers and
up on the ramparts followed suit.' The reward for his vocal
exertion was a certificate signed by the Lady President of the
Festival Committee.

This glamour was the stuff that Manfred Baumann was
seeking to capitalise on in his *Everyman* thriller. Familiar,
popular locations and events invariably set the scene for his
murder cases. A case in a later book is set in the Hellbrunn
Palace summer residence, where a well-known socialite is slain
amid the famous fountains. And in another, an opera diva
drops dead midway through a performance. And not just any
opera singer, but the Queen of the Night; nor just anywhere,
but in the Salzburg Festival Hall; nor just at any old time, but
in the middle of the premiere of Mozart's *Magic Flute*.

Baumann's role model, he frankly admits, is Donna Leon.
In her books, too, the star is basically the city of Venice, like
some imposing theatre backdrop in front of which the characters must play their parts. Without this, he wouldn't find
Leon's stories themselves nearly so gripping, with the possible exception of her character Commissario Brunetti's fourth
case, *Vendetta*. His aim likewise, he says, is to bring the city
to life in his books, even though in the process he may often

teeter on the edge of, and even sometimes slip into, cliché.

He quite consciously plays with clichés, in stories that could in truth only take place here in Salzburg and not, say, in Linz or New York. The shimmering summer heat of the city, with people in evening dress mingling with backpackers in T-shirts: that's Baumann's Salzburg.

The author also freely accepts that some readers will find that he's laid it on a bit thick when, for instance, in the case of the *Mozart-Ball Plot*, a naked and extremely well-endowed Mozart impersonator is found dead, murdered with poisoned Mozart-balls – and in the house where the composer was born, of all places. As a counterpoint to all these Salzburg clichés, there are also quite a few instances in his novels where he takes issue with the place, referring to 'vultures in Loden coats', say, or Salzburgers bellyaching about tourists, or the shamelessly inflated prices on restaurant menus. He also criticises the 'Old Town Commission' – a body that exists in reality and whose agenda is to preserve the historic cityscape – as being fundamentally hostile to enterprise, a common complaint against it. There's talk of sewer rats, the construction mafia and a coterie of cronies around the mayor. In one of his novels, the beggars of Salzburg play a key role. And Merana's girlfriend gets involved with the Citizens' Party – in a city where a grassroots citizens' movement really is active in local politics. Groups such as this proved a decisive factor in the genesis of the Austrian Green Movement.

However, Baumann firmly rejects any suggestion that all this is just a way of unburdening himself of the sort of criticism that he would never have been allowed to voice so subjectively in his former career as a journalist with the official state broadcaster ORF. Besides, his critical forays are only brief, occasional moments that cast light into a dark corner far removed from the glossy image of Salzburg but then allow this image to shine forth all the more brightly. Baumann's character Merana is a world away from the milieu of sweeping social criticism and gritty real-life politics set against a backcloth of financial crisis, corruption and intrigue that, say, the writer Petros Markaris has his Commissar Kostas Charitos operate within in Athens. Baumann lets the Baroque idyll predominate, and briefly spatters it with blood.

'A Salzburg Crime Thriller' is the byline on the cover of Baumann's books. So you instantly know where the crime is committed and solved. Admittedly, the author is neither the first nor the only writer to use the city as a setting for plumbing the depths of the human soul.

The most well-known of them is undoubtedly Wolf Haas, whose 1999 thriller *Silentium!*, which was also filmed, stirred up a hornets' nest of sexual abuse in boarding schools. And who in Salzburg would be at all surprised that private investigator Simon Brenner meets up with a secretary of the Salzburg Festival in the novel?

Likewise, the Graz-born writer Manfred Koch also wrote several crime novels with a Salzburg connection. These are grim tales, enigmatic psychograms and thrillers which, even if sometimes a bit over the top, are 'aimed at hardcore crime fans, victims of thriller overkill and dyed-in-the-wool haters of crime fiction alike', as he himself characterises one of his works on his homepage.

Like Baumann, Franz Zeller also has an ORF background. *Herzlos* (*Heartless*), which appeared in 2009, was his first Salzburg-set crime novel. In this work, Chief Inspector Franco Moll is called upon to solve a series of unexplained deaths in a Salzburg cardiac clinic. Zeller is also well aware of the power of particular crime-scene locations for novels; his work *Sieben Letzte Worte* (*Seven Last Words*) featured a body being washed down the Almkanal from the fortress.

Ursula Poznanski, who has already won many awards for her writing, has returned to Salzburg time and again to find settings for her thrillers, though not the glamorous locations. In *Blinde Vögel* (*Blind Birds*), the first task facing her detective is to identify two bodies discovered at a Salzburg campsite, while in *Fünf* (*Five*) a woman is killed after falling from a crag outside Salzburg.

By contrast, the latest work by Tatjana Kruse takes place in the heart of the city. Shady characters and any amount of Mozart-balls dominate the scene as a whole series of opera singers are murdered in *Bei Zugabe Mord!* (*Death at the Encore!*).

University lecturer Max Oban from Upper Austria, meanwhile, has put his detective Paul Peck on the case. Titles like *Mozarts kleine Mordmusik* (*Mozart's Little Murder Music*) and *Tod in Salzburg* (*Death in Salzburg*) leave one in no doubt as to where these works are set.

No question, Salzburg has also got pulling power in crime

fiction. Leopoldskron Palace, the Mozartsteg and the Festival Hall are all featured by writers. And in addition to policemen, private investigators and even in one case an opera soprano rack their brains to solve crimes committed on the mean streets of Salzburg.

Like Charitos, and like Maigret, Brunetti and Wallander, Baumann's detective is a 'Commissar', although no such rank exists in the Austrian CID. 'It just sounds better than Major or Colonel,' admits the author. Martin Merana comes from the Pinzgau region; in other words, he isn't an urban Salzburger. Nor is Baumann, he comes from Hallein. And his commissar is a totally fictional character, not like in the fiction of Martin Walker, who modelled his Bruno Courrèges – who as the only policeman in Saint Denis in Périgord is at the same time automatically the *chef de police* – on a real officer of the law. But like Bruno and his longing for Pamela, Merana too is prone to complicated love affairs. Nonetheless, he plays things by the book and is punctilious to a fault, and if need be he will ditch any prospect of a romantic moment when duty calls. His cases are woven according to a classic pattern: a spectacular murder, several potential perpetrators, a number of suspects with a possible motive, and various subplots including insights into the commissar's private life. Intrigues, jealousy, alcohol, awkward artistic types, anxious festival organisers. In the end, the detective's instinct or an inspired 'hunch' leads him to the culprit, who up to that point has played something of a minor role in the plot.

In the process, one learns a lot about the surroundings,

the city, some of which is made up, though a lot is accurate. But what of it? Well, it clearly interests Salzburgers as well. Baumann is surprised that natives of the city also read his books. They were conceived rather with fans of Salzburg in mind, those who have a certain insider's knowledge though not in any great depth. People who had fallen in love with Salzburg were his target readership, in the same way as he sees himself as a Venice-lover. That's why he chose as a setting for his debut novel the striking location of the cathedral square. He constructs all his plots from the setting – who could have been done to death there, and why? Only then does he start to flesh out the characters. By the time he begins writing, the plot, the sequence of events and all the connections have been carefully designed. For some authors, the plot only comes together in the act of writing. Not for Baumann; he knows who the perp is right from the outset, and even the title has been fixed long since, so when he comes to put pen to paper, as it were, things go at quite a lick. He can finish a book in two to three weeks, working up to sixteen hours a day, and all straight through in one hit. And then it's off to the publisher.

Once that's done, he has plenty of time to devote to public readings and the cabaret group he performs in, but also to mulling over where the next crime might be committed. It's certainly advisable from a commercial point of view to stick with the same genre and the same city. He's well aware of the danger of repetition when he's expected to turn out a book a year. He has broken with this formula once already, because a television producer wanted to film one of his stories, not in the city but at the Krimml Waterfalls. So the TV script was completed even before the novel *Drachenjungfrau* (*Dragon Virgin*), and Merana was required to do his sleuthing in the sticks. An excursion for the filming, then.

For the moment, though, he has given his commissar a well-earned rest and is mulling over other genres. Involving murders committed, say, in a herbarium somewhere, or one set at Christmas. But the Salzburg Commissar Merana will be reactivated at some stage. As a former television journalist, his creator will once again think first in terms of images and plots. And whether the setting turns out to be St Sebastian's cemetery, the fortress or an atmospheric, kitschy Advent Market, there's no shortage of locations in Salzburg where Death will rear its truly ugly head once more.

12

Building Bridges

*Only the icy waters bear witness when
love chains itself to the railings*

IT HARDLY BEARS THINKING about that vows of love
might one day end up in the crusher. When something
that was meant to last for all time is shown to be transient.
Love endures for all eternity, people insist when they are in
love, and at some stage they get the urge to make an outward
show of it. No sooner has a kiss stolen in the shadows grown
accustomed to the light of day than it craves the limelight.
And what theatricality can compare with the setting of a
Baroque city against the backdrop of a mighty fortress, in
itself a symbol of permanence and immortality?

And so a closely woven mesh of stainless-steel wires is a
place tailor-made for pledging eternal love and fixing it there
in perpetuity in the form of brass and iron. Over time, the
balustrade of the Makartsteg, the pedestrian bridge, has
become festooned with shiny, colourful love padlocks in
their thousands. They already look like they weigh more than
the railings they're attached to.

A bridge is frequently required to carry heavy weights. Structural engineers calculate its load-bearing capacity. But how to measure the combined weight of all those promises of undying love? Even the city's politicians and municipal works officials scratch their heads at that one – and let the lovebirds carry on. For the time being, anyhow.

When the first padlocks began to appear on the then brand-new walkway, the city authorities had them nipped off with bolt cutters, without more ado. 'To start with, I had no idea what it all meant,' admits a smiling Claudia Schmidt, who was the councillor overseeing the city works department at the time. However, 'after looking into it a bit more, I thought to myself, what a charming idea! Salzburg's rather fuddy-duddy, to be honest.' Not all local authority employees shared their leader's view, though, and so they secured from her the proviso that these tokens of love should not be too heavy and that the steel mesh was not to be damaged in any way when attaching them, lest this constitute a hazard to pedestrians crossing the bridge.

Indeed, that's something that's already happened in Paris, where a section of the balustrade on the Pont des Arts gave way under the weight of lovers' padlocks. But because even this failed to deter lovers from indulging their habit, in July 2015 the railings were dismantled and stripped of all the padlocks before being reinstalled. Old love was cast onto the scrapheap to make way for the new. That's how life goes sometimes. In Rome, too, the city authorities have come to regard this romanticism in metal as a scourge and have started to remove padlocks from the Ponte Milvio and other bridges. In fact, it was on the Milvian Bridge over the Tiber that this particular romantic ritual first began. The practice was made popular by the Italian writer Federico Moccia in his 2006 novel *Ho voglia di te* (*I Want You*). In the meantime, the craze has taken hold in several cities around the world, while in Rome it is rumoured that a fine of up to 250 euros might soon be imposed on people caught attaching padlocks to bridges. This would mean that love would once more be forced to blossom in secret. Which is where it feels most at ease, after all.

There's no talk of such measures in Salzburg yet. The colourful glittering wall of padlocks in front of the photogenic backdrop has long since become a favoured location for photos in its own right. With a bit of luck, you might even discover padlocks with messages in Arabic or Far Eastern characters. Love is international.

Sheepishly, a young lad rummages in the pocket of his blue jacket and pulls out a shiny red object of the sort that you can buy in several shops hereabouts. They're labelled as 'Love Locks' in window displays. And they come supplied with two keys. The girl in jeans next to him presses herself against the mesh and tries to shield him from inquisitive glances. It seems like some silent ritual, as their metal declaration of love clicks quietly shut on a free spot on the railings. Their eyes meet, expressing a sacred yearning. They press their lips together but break off abruptly for a moment so they can both watch the little key falling through space before hitting the waters of the Salzach, which will never give it up again, and then kiss once more. In an attempt to deflate any seriousness, they burst out laughing intermittently, but only for a few seconds at a time.

My question as to what significance the ritual has for them shatters the intimate idyll. Even so, they're keen to talk, and later we repair to the Café Bazar for a cup of tea.

They met in the Rupertus bookshop in Salzburg, when they both reached for the same book. A brief touching of hands, a twinge, a spark. They both went on to buy the book in question.

She's called Amaya, her friends call her Aya. In Japanese that means 'night rain', but also 'beloved daughter'. What do those two things have to do with one another? She just smiles bashfully at this; it's anyone's guess. Her tight black hair is cut short. He'd prefer it if it were longer. He hasn't shaved for a few days – she doesn't actually like that, she says, giving him a smile. She's studying piano at the Mozarteum, and she reckons she's been really lucky to get a place at this famous institute. That makes it sound like she's already guaranteed a glittering international career, but that isn't the case, she knows that. Even among the elite there's a crush, and only a tiny number of people can make it to the very top. Now it's the vacation she's going back home again, to Osaka, after a long absence. Four weeks in Japan will be a long time for the young couple to be apart. The metal object hanging on the mesh of the Makartsteg is meant to vouch for the fact that it's only going to be a temporary separation. Andreas bought it and inscribed their initials on it with a waterproof marker pen. He knows that lots of the padlocks have been engraved, but as a student he couldn't afford that. And what does it matter anyway? Even as it stands they'll be able to find the guarantor of their love on the walkway again and then be back in the Here and Now. As a prospective lawyer, he shows his pragmatic side.

This prompts me to ask, purely pragmatically, what the second key that came with the lock is for. Will it be put away in a drawer somewhere, as collateral so to speak, so that the padlock can be opened again if need be in the event that their relationship comes to an end? – What kind of a question is that? It's sacrilege! No way that's ever going to happen, and besides, they threw the spare key away immediately after autographing the lock. They're going to hook up again after Amaya's holiday and then they'll start planning their future together, Andreas says. I believe the two of them, in the way one is desperate to put faith in all lovers.

For surely not one of the thousands of couples consider the prospect of their ardour cooling or of separation when – either furtively and clandestinely or loud and joyously – they snap their little padlocks shut on the bridge balustrade and cast the keys into the waters below, as if banishing from the world forever the code that could break their tender bond.

Not that the Makartsteg hasn't, over the course of its short history, already seen its share of catastrophes, and not just small private ones either but major public ones. Such as the tourist boat *Amadeus* capsizing during record flooding in August 2002. The vessel had only been in service a few months, taking sightseers out for a view of the old city from the Salzach, when it was swamped by the river in full spate and sank at its moorings. Pictures of the stricken *Amadeus* even appeared on the front page of *The New York Times*, making the little boat famous the world over. After being salvaged and extensively repaired, the excursion boat, with its nine-man crew, has once again become a very popular attraction. Although it has a draught of only 40 centimetres, it can still find itself unable to set sail when the river is low. Especially in autumn, the water level of the Salzach can sometimes fall to below 80 centimetres.

Under no circumstances should the river's current be underestimated. It rises in the Kitzbühel Alps and forces itself through fantastic gorges like, say, the famous Salzach-öfen and remains dangerous even in its lower reaches as it flows through Salzburg. Even in the early summer, the Salzach still carries a great deal of meltwater. Some years ago, a young man who wanted to cool off and tried to swim across the river by the Makartsteg was swept away and his body was not retrieved for several days. Anyone who accidentally tumbles into the swollen river has an even slimmer chance of survival.

That aside, eager spectators always gather at the bridge whenever a visiting dignitary is due to make an appearance. Even the former Turkish president Abdullah Gül didn't want to pass up an opportunity for a photo-call on the Makartsteg during his state visit to Austria in 2011. For the elegant, sweeping pedestrian crossing has become a firm fixture in VIPs' sightseeing tours of the city. Other than that, it's a heavily used shortcut between two parts of the city. For every city that sits on a river, bridges are vital arteries. In Salzburg, the Makartsteg is for pedestrians what the Staatsbrücke is for cars. The bridge is named after the painter Hans Makart, who became renowned for his sumptuous large-format works, his legendary studio parties and the late nineteenth-century style of interior design created for the Viennese *haute bourgeoisie* that bears his name, principally in the imperial capital, though he was born in Salzburg. There is still a plaque commemorating him at the Mirabell Palace, where he was born into the nobility – which would remain his milieu throughout his life – in May 1840. He only lived to the age of forty-four but even during his lifetime, in 1879, the square in Salzburg originally known as Hannibalplatz was rechristened Makartplatz.

The bridge that runs from this square over to the left bank of the Salzach was only built much later. The current crossing is the third bridge to stand here. The first Makartsteg was an offspring of the Art Nouveau movement, constructed in 1905, just two years after the Mozartsteg, which still survives in its original form. This latter crossing, which stands upstream of the Staatsbrücke, has now been eclipsed by the Makartsteg. Its iron-framework structure is somewhat reminiscent of the work of Gustave Eiffel, and an archway at the entrance to the bridge is emblazoned with a cast-iron plaque bearing the date 1903. Nowadays, the great majority of visitors to this bridge are either residents who happen to live nearby or dyed-in-the-wool Mozart fans.

In contrast, the Makartsteg has become a pedestrian highway. The old Art Nouveau bridge there was taken down in 1967 and replaced by a new swing bridge. However, the vibrations caused by the footfall of some 20,000 pedestrians a day weakened the structure to such an extent that it had to be closed in 2000 and dismantled. The current bridge is made of concrete, with its curving form – the work of the Salzburg architectural practice Halle 1 – resting on just a single pier, while the railings are in stainless steel. The whole thing is designed to last for many decades. Even though we know full well, ever since the 1965 hit by German singer-songwriter Drafi Deutscher, that 'Marble, stone and iron break' ('Marmor, Stein und Eisen bricht'). The only thing that doesn't, supposedly, is our love.

You instinctively ask yourself whether all those who have ever padlocked their love to a set of bridge railings are still an item. No one knows. You can't assume that it is the case. But equally it's not surprising that people sometimes come to check things out on the spot.

Dusk has almost fallen, and there aren't many people about any more when a couple position themselves at one part of the railing and start picking up one lock after another and scrutinising them intently. They're clearly looking for a particular one. You need a lot of patience for that. They either don't notice that they are being observed from a discreet distance, or it doesn't bother them. They don't appear to know exactly where they should be looking. Or rather they've forgotten, as it later transpires. After endless minutes searching, they pause. They stand up slowly and gaze into the distance, up at the fortress. And then they proceed silently on their way, walking beside one another, until one hand seeks out the other's. Arriving on the bank, they initially fight shy of responding to my questions. Yes, they finally concede, they were looking for their love lock, which they'd put on the bridge years ago. Why? Ah, well ... they hesitate, before telling me what had kept the thought in their heads all those years. Just like the railings had kept hold of the padlock.

Back then, many years ago, they had been among the very first people to attach this token of their relationship to the mesh, in dead secrecy, in the same way their relationship was totally hush-hush. Their love was illicit, because it was completely out of the question. She wasn't a free agent back then and was wearing another man's ring, and for that reason neither of them want to tell me their names. Their world had ultimately fallen apart thanks to that ring. He'd realised it would be that way from very early on, despite hoping against hope. But a burning love isn't deterred by the prospect of one day being left empty-handed, he says, quoting the French writer Stendhal. As Stendhal of all people must have known, since his Mathilde would be the one great, unrequited love of his life.

A person who is infatuated never asks what the difference between love and infatuation is. It was only logical that they should go their separate ways, but their thoughts remained intact. As did the padlock on the bridge balustrade. A chance encounter in the very town that had brought them together in the first place all those years ago had now reawakened all their old feelings. Including their heartache. She's still got her wedding ring on. And now he's wearing one too.

13

Shoebox with Don Giovanni

A farsighted museum

EVERY MORNING AT eight o'clock, Beate gets on the bus. The number 7 takes her from Lehen to the Staatsbrücke. From there it's just a short step into the Old Town on the right bank of the river. Lehen isn't exactly the most exclusive part of Salzburg, but rather a low-rent residential neighbourhood, in so far as you can ever talk in terms of cheap accommodation in Salzburg.

There was a time when the main attraction of the district was the stadium, formerly the home ground of SV Austria Salzburg. You could watch their games from the windows of the houses overlooking the pitch. But in the meantime, the former football club has been swallowed up by Red Bull and relocated to a new stadium near the motorway. A new Austria Salzburg was founded and the old Lehen ground torn down to make room for a housing complex and a library. The move has prompted endless debates, just like everything else concerned with building projects in Salzburg.

That makes no odds to Beate; she's got a flat in Lehen and a job in a shoe shop in the Old Town. She still enjoys showing customers the latest shoe styles, even when tourists have her dashing to and from the stockroom seven times just in order to try on yet another pair, and maybe the same one in a different size, and then end up buying nothing after all. Because they view shopping as a recreational activity, as an opportunity to experience something without necessarily spending any money in the process. Whatever the customer wants, Beate has to keep returning to the stockroom because it's not the done thing in the shop where she works to stack shoes of all sizes in boxes in the retail area. Her boss doesn't like it – those stacks of boxes are for the discount stores, not for her, she's always saying. So, in this shop all you ever see are individual pairs neatly arranged on swish glass shelves, waiting for customers.

When Beate heads home again in the evening, she walks down the Linzergasse to the Platzl square next to the Staatsbrücke in order to catch the bus in the direction of Lehen. From there, standing by the little waterspouts that spring straight up out of the ground, she has in her field of vision a huge shoebox, and it annoys her that, before it was built, no one thought to ask her boss, who would surely have raised an objection. On its exterior is the legend 'Museum der Moderne' ('Museum of Modern Art'). The shoe-shop assistant has never been inside; she's pretty certain it's not her kind of thing. But sometimes customers in the shop will start going on about what an amazing view there is from up there and saying that once you get inside the museum, it's not at all like a box. Quite the opposite, in fact. Spacious galleries are linked by a high stairwell that's flooded with light, while the rear elevation of the staircase penetrates the external stone-clad façade of the building like a single, tall shaft. The side of the museum that faces the city looks like a bland, smooth, unbroken surface, but this impression is surely only down to the fact that from below, thanks to a terrace that's been built in front, you can't see the large ground-floor glass entrance doors, behind which there is an excellent restaurant. It's called the M32, the 'M' standing for Mönchsberg.

This terrace affords a panoramic view over the whole of the old city. The Kapuzinerberg on the far side of the Salzach looks close enough to reach out and touch, while to the left of it, much further away, stands the pilgrimage church of Maria Plain, behind which the wide plain of the Flachgau, which runs right up to the border with Bavaria, opens out. To the right, immediately below you as you look down, you can see straight down the entire length of the Hofstallgasse. You can almost make out who's entering the Festival Hall wearing what dress, or who's inclining their head to sip a beer outside the Restaurant Triangel.

The Mönchsberg was formerly the site of the Grand Café Winkler, a dance venue of great opulence and a popular sightseeing destination, not least because it once housed the famous circular panorama of Salzburg painted by the early nineteenth-century artist Johann Michael Sattler. Benita Ferrero-Waldner, who was the Austrian Foreign Minister from

2000 to 2004, still has fond memories of how dances used to be held here 'every Saturday evening for months on end' when she was a young girl. The Winkler was also home to a casino, which has since moved to Kleßheim Castle, much to the annoyance of those responsible for the city's finances. For Kleßheim is part of the neighbouring municipality of Wals-Siezenheim, already one of the wealthiest districts in Austria, which is now in addition raking in the local gaming taxes levied on the casino. As for the Sattler Panorama, which is painted on a canvas measuring 125 square metres and is a painstaking depiction of the city and its environs dating from 1829, it has been beautifully renovated after surviving a chequered past, including being carted around the whole of Europe, and is now displayed in a purpose-built building in the Neue Residenz Palace. The Café Winkler, with its broad glazed frontage and water tower behind, formed something of an architectural whole. Viewed from below, it looked like a rather squat castle with a watchtower, and the colourful sunshades outside on the terrace were an additional draw, tempting you to take the late-nineteenth-century electrically powered lift that ran up the cliff face, leaving the Baroque roofscape of the town far below as you ascended. The lift, which was a great attraction in its own right, comprised two cabins that ran up and down the escarpment on slender steel rails, and was at the time of its construction the tallest in the whole of Europe, at 60 metres. It was also rumoured to have been the model for the elevators that were subsequently installed in American skyscrapers.

'And now all there is up there is that shoebox,' grumbled Beate and many of her fellow Salzburgers when the new Museum of Modern Art first opened its doors in 2004 with an exhibition on the theme of light featuring several internationally renowned artists. Since then, the building has sat enthroned on the Mönchsberg in a laid-back, matter-of-fact kind of way, like a second fortress counterpointing the original castle with its contemporary architectural statement.

Even just the plans for its construction brought long and heated debates in their wake, like the tail of a comet, and these were far more emotional than those surrounding the demolition of the Lehen stadium. After all, this site was immeasurably more prominent and sensitive.

'It's something of a miracle that it's here at all,' ventures Sabine Breitwieser with a mischievous smile. A native of Upper Austria, she has been in post as director of the Museum of Modern Art since 2013, prior to which she was chief curator of media and performance art at MoMA in New York. At the time it was being built, however, she followed the controversy surrounding the Salzburg museum from her then-home in Vienna. I meet her in her small office, with its exposed concrete ceiling, and a view not over the city but instead facing the woods behind the museum. Her work station with computer screen is a standing desk, and on the wall are some poster designs for upcoming exhibitions.

Recently, her institution staged one about building projects that had been planned in Salzburg over the course of the centuries but which had never come to fruition. To be fair, concedes Breitwieser as we sit chatting on a yellow settee designed by Franz West, it's worth noting that you could put on something of the sort in any city you care to name. 'Yet the overall look of this city is sacrosanct. Its image has been frozen in time by edict, so to speak.' That makes it difficult for it to properly meet the demands of modern life. And yet for the most part, she says, the Guggenheim Foundation's plans for a museum in the city that were once up for discussion wouldn't even have impacted the city's appearance. The star Austrian architect Hans Hollein had drawn up plans for a museum to be constructed inside the Mönchsberg. The idea for such a building had been around since the 1970s. It was intended to become a European centre for the visual arts and to be a home within Central Europe for the Guggenheim Museum. Notwithstanding its existing, highly attractive sites in Venice and New York, the Guggenheim Foundation was quite prepared to open a museum in Salzburg as well. With the success story of the Guggenheim in Bilbao in mind, the proponents of the scheme sought to build a consensus among the city and the province of Salzburg and the government of the Austrian Republic. But in the end that's precisely what they failed to achieve.

Hollein's blueprint was long since complete and had garnered several accolades. The plan was to open the museum in the 'Mozart Year' of 2006. Studies put the projected annual number of visitors at 650,000. They would have entered the Mönchsberg complex at the bottom, in the city, and a large spiral walkway would have given onto a series of rooms and recesses. Visitors would have corkscrewed their way up the hollowed-out hill until they reached the large main exhibition hall. For fifteen years, Salzburg was convulsed by the ongoing debate about this project and more generally about how the arts could and should be experienced within this city of culture. At the time, the construction costs were put at around 100 million euros. Not exactly a trifling sum for a building where practically none of the almost 7,000 square metres of exhibition space would be visible from the outside.

Several years later, the architect Wilhelm Holzbauer, one of the few people who have managed to turn a project sited in a prominent location in Salzburg into reality in recent years, observed critically in a television interview: 'You just have to consider that the rock is full of water, which will seep in all over the place unless you take measures to stop it. The building would have become a concrete cylinder with a hill behind it. The operating costs would have been unimaginable.' Then again, others took the view that the sheer pulling power of the museum in the mountain would have long since paid for itself and that the technical challenges of building it could well have been surmounted in the twenty-first century. Besides, the innards of the Mönchsberg had long since been scooped out in order to create large underground car parks.

Nonetheless, the project was abandoned before even a single spadeful of earth was turned. It foundered on lack of funding, but even more so on the failure of those who should have promoted it to close ranks and give it the impetus it required. But what also killed it was the concern that

Salzburg might suddenly acquire too much exhibition space. For at the same time the second museum up on top of the Mönchsberg was already taking firm shape.

For a long time, the Rupertinum Museum had been bursting at the seams. Located in the city centre, between the cathedral square and the Festival Hall, it dates back to the mid-fourteenth century and for many centuries of its history was a seminary, and thereafter a student hall of residence. It has only been a museum of modern art since 1983, and the early Baroque building soon became too cramped for this purpose. The annexe on the Mönchsberg was meant to rectify this situation.

And so the austere new building was planned, based on designs by the Munich architectural practice of Friedrich Hoff Zwink, with 2,300 square metres of gallery space for art of the twentieth and twenty-first centuries. Would both buildings really have been too much? At a stage when the excavators should already have started breaking ground up on the hill, down in the town they were still wrangling about potential synergy between the two projects. City and provincial politicians quarrelled vociferously, occasionally egged on by the central government in Vienna. While the province of Salzburg voted in favour of the Museum of Modern Art, the city continued to withhold planning permission. A series of new studies were designed to foster cooperation between the two projects, as well as with major museums in Vienna, but by then the atmosphere was no longer conducive to such an approach. Consequently, the larger museum inside the mountain remained just a vision, while the smaller one on top of the hill became a reality. The result was our shoebox.

Sabine Breitwieser isn't crying over spilt milk. She maintains she doesn't miss the Guggenheim Museum in the hill as a potential partner. 'But our entrance still isn't finished. Plus too little thought has been given to how large objects can be brought up here to the museum.' That's another chapter in the story of unbuilt Salzburg.

The only way of getting to the museum, if you don't fancy making the rather arduous climb on foot, is by using one of the three lifts that run inside the cliff. There is a road up to the top, but it's narrow and steep, as well as being tricky for larger vehicles to negotiate and treacherous in the winter. When the museum was under construction a wider temporary bridge had to be erected especially, and it was due to be taken down again at the end of the building work. 'It's still there, but it'll most likely soon fall down of its own accord,' says the director, though she's relieved it's still standing for the present. Interim solutions have a way of clinging on for a long time, as is the case with the lift too. Its lower station is situated on the Gstättengasse, where a single row of houses still presses up against the cliff face, and where the little buildings convey an impression of what old Salzburg was once like. There are a couple of shops in this small alleyway, and one or two inns, but otherwise it's all old townhouses. And between these is the entrance to the secular catacombs of Salzburg, leading to an underground car park and to a long tunnel through which you can walk in the dry all the way to the Festival Hall. And through which you can get to the lift, although you have to pay extra for that.

Breitwieser would like there to be an easily accessible and attractive entrance to the museum. As originally planned, in fact, with a far more spectacular 55-metre-high glass panoramic lift ascending the face of the escarpment. That would have been a worthy successor to the old external lift that operated until 1947, taking people up to the Café Winkler. However, this project, designed by the architects Delugan Meissl, has so far remained on the drawing board, like so much else here.

It was also originally envisaged that the institution on top of the Mönchsberg would become home to one of the most significant private collections of classic modern art, namely that of the Liechtenstein lawyer Herbert Batliner. One of the central arguments of those who lobbied for the museum's construction was that it would be able to secure this collection for display in Salzburg in perpetuity. However, the wrangling over the museum evidently proved too much in the long run for this wealthy patron of the arts, so he withdrew from the scheme, and nowadays his important exhibits, covering 130 years of art history from Monet to Picasso, grace the galleries of the Albertina in Vienna instead.

Even so, the Modern Art Museum's holdings are vast. Thanks to an endowment from the gallery owner Friedrich Welz, its core comprises a wealth of graphic works by Oskar Kokoschka, Paul Klee, Gustav Klimt, Herbert Boeckl, Alfred Kubin and Fritz Wotruba. This graphic work has since been supplemented by numerous paintings and sculptures, particularly by contemporary Austrian artists including Gunter Damisch, Franz Ringel and Hubert Schmalix, plus many sketches and photographs. 'That's several thousand works all told, though not all of them are important,' says the gallery director. Much of this material will first have to be evaluated. And now, in addition to all these, there are some 2,500 pictures from the Generali Foundation, a first-class modern collection which accords perfectly with the director's conception of the museum. For she has decreed that it must 'reposition' itself. Her aim is to raise its international profile by pointing forward from contemporary art into the future and not just providing a historical perspective. It's all very unsettling. 'Art is meant to be unsettling,' she maintains. 'Sure, there are some people who will find what I'm doing dreadful, but others will be happy that we're promoting ourselves more.'

The first thing will be to build a depository for all these works. That's another plan that has not yet been realised. Plus the museum needs to attract more visitors.

A concrete surface in the stairwell still bears traces of lettering spelling out the name 'Georg Baselitz' – an advertisement for an earlier exhibition. Big names draw the public. Whether the visionaries of the art-gallery world can also do so remains to be seen. 'Visitor numbers are stable at just over a hundred thousand a year,' says Breitwieser. But even within Salzburg, her institution is in competition with numerous other museums, let alone all the many galleries. For instance, the magnificent showpiece rooms of the Alte Residenz, the medieval seat of the bishops of Salzburg, are a sight to behold.

The cathedral quarter gives visitors an insight into the power and majesty of the prince-archbishops. Meanwhile, the Salzburg Museum on Mozartplatz charts the development of the region since the time of the Celts and the Middle Ages, and the Natural History Museum has exhibits ranging from the dinosaurs to space exploration, with other visitor attractions being Mozart's birthplace and the house where he lived, while anyone with an interest in great minds will be bound to take a detour to see the Georg-Trakl-House memorial site on Waagplatz. The fortress naturally has its own museum, and on the other side of the old city, on the Kapuzinerberg, you can follow in the footsteps of Stefan Zweig. Meanwhile, those who are after less cerebral pursuits can visit museums dedicated to brewing, folklore, toys and even Christmas. And that's not an end to the list by any means.

When Beate the shoe-shop assistant looks up at the Mönchsberg from the Platzl by the Staatsbrücke, she can't see that the museum's façade of local Untersberg marble isn't actually devoid of all decoration. Here and there, the panels of stone cladding have vertical slots cut into them, at irregular intervals. It's said that a computer program determined the positioning of these slots by transposing the rhythmic structure of an aria from Mozart's opera *Don Giovanni*. It's not at all easy to see how this works in practice; perhaps the story was just a clever marketing ploy on the part of the architect, but in any event it was a nod in the direction of the city's presiding *genius loci*. In Salzburg, even a museum of modern art can't avoid referencing Mozart.

14

Pricey Paving

Rubbing shoulders with the super-rich.
Compactness comes at a cost

IT'S TAKEN A LONG TIME. Interminably long for many
people, but now it's finally in place, the new road surface on
the Getreidegasse. It's often claimed that Salzburg has Italian
flair. It may well be true that there is indeed something very
Italian about the paving in the streets and alleyways of the Old
Town. In so far as it warrants the term, that is – it's a tarmac
surface that's been patched and repatched a dozen times. Not
to mention the presence of kerbstones, even though a separate
pavement isn't necessary because the area has been pedestri-
anised for years. A streetscape designed to break your ankles.
The noble Getreidegasse has long since been deemed unwor-
thy of such a mess. In the other part of the old city across the
river, after many years of protracted debate and just as long a
planning phase, granite flagstones have finally also been laid
in the Linzergasse, albeit initially only in the lower half of the
street. Good things take time.

In the Getreidegasse, too, the sensible first step was to repair and renovate the 100-year-old sewers and other utilities.

Once that had been done, the top surface of Berbing granite could be laid – the 'cooled blood of the earth', as one supplier describes the material in its promotional literature. It comes from the corner where three countries meet: Austria, Germany and Czechia. The resurfacing work began at the Alter Markt and was only completed after two excruciating years of upheaval. Michael Handl, the boss of the city works department, reveals that this phase of the project cost almost two million euros.

Pricey paving, then. But undeniably handsome.

The same goes for the city as a whole. The housing market price index shows Salzburg as being the most expensive city in the whole of Austria. On average, you need to shell out more than 4,800 euros per square metre for a freehold flat. That's far more than in Vienna, where the increase in house prices has been ultimately far less. And fully three times as much as in St Pölten. Okay, St Pölten is hardly Salzburg. Here, the demand and the prices continue to rise steeply, as they always have. For one thing, its geographical and geopolitical location is ideal. It's close to the mountains, close to Italy, relatively close to the sea, very close to Germany and within easy reach of the lake holiday resorts of the Salzkammergut region. It's not far to go skiing, sailing or swimming, or to play a round of golf. And it's just a step away if you want to attend a concert or go to the theatre. Another reason for

Salzburg's priciness is the limited space available. The mountains surrounding the city permit little expansion. There's Gaisberg in the east, Untersberg in the south, and between them Mönchsberg and Kapuzinerberg, and right in the heart of the city the fortress bluff too.

That's what drives up the cost of existing housing. There are virtually no plots for expansion. In scarcely any other city are green spaces guarded as jealously as they are here.

Since 1985, Salzburg's urban environment has been under the special protection of a green-belt statute. In it, the city's political authorities have given an undertaking that they will permit no further reclassification of green areas as land for development. Citizens' action committees were responsible for this policy and monitor its observance. The instigators of the original initiative were two city councillors from a local residents' political grouping: the insurance agent Johannes Voggenhuber and the actor Herbert Fux.

They became active in the wake of the spectacular occupation of the Danube flood plain near Hainburg by people protesting against the planned construction of a power station, which had dominated Austrian politics in the winter of 1984. After participating in the fierce debates about environmental protection that raged in Vienna and Salzburg, just a year later the two men encountered one another again as delegates to the National Assembly. And so it was that the future eminent European politician and the man with the craggy face who specialised in playing villains on screen became the trailblazers of the Austrian Green movement. Anyone who is fortunate enough to live in a green-belt area in Salzburg that cannot be built on has them to thank for their pleasant surroundings.

Thereafter, the political slogan beloved of regional planners has been 'housing consolidation'. The global trend towards urbanisation in general and the attractiveness of Salzburg in particular has led to a significant growth in the satellite communities surrounding the city. The transport infrastructure, though, has lagged badly behind.

As a result, the city itself has remained manageably small. This, together with its cultural offer, makes it a very attractive place to live for those who can afford it. In addition, Salzburg is easy to get to. Motorways flank the city to the north and the west, acting at one and the same time as municipal boundaries and as heavily used feeder roads. The airport here is close to the city centre, and passengers virtually never experience long delays.

And finally, where can you enjoy a more exhilarating breakfast than, say, on the roof-terrace of the Hotel Stein, looking at the perfect old-city panorama, and with the prospect of being able to visit almost all of its attractions on foot?

This all makes it wonderfully fertile territory for estate agents. The leading light among them is Alexander Kurz, a native son of the city, a genuine Salzburger in other words, whom you can occasionally find dressed in lederhosen, though his business is not confined to Salzburg by any means. First and foremost, his speciality is in highly priced luxury properties – villas and country houses throughout the whole of Austria. He's also got thirty-odd castles on his books.

His office is on the edge of one of these undeveloped green-belt zones, with a clear view of the fortress. In his sonorous voice, he explains the true worth of valuable property. Birds of a feather flock together. And so it's the wealth already present around the Salzach that draws other wealthy people here. 'They don't have to fear they'll encounter any unpleasantness here,' Kurz says. Accordingly, the last thing he wants for the city and for his business is for anyone to go round stirring up the politics of envy. Some years ago, he was able to sell 'a really lovely property' in Salzburg to a client from Germany with a considerable fortune, he tells me. And just like that, this guy then goes and relocates the headquarters of his firm, with more than 26,000 employees, to Austria too. So securing all those additional tax revenues for the country. But that kind of thing has become more difficult of late. The market segment for the super-rich has seen a downturn since politicians started talking about wealth taxes and various kinds of property levy.

But even below the level of the super-rich, there's plenty of business to be done. While still expensive by most people's standards, 'average' freehold properties are very much in demand. As second homes too, though technically that's not permitted. People just like to spend a free weekend now and then in Salzburg. According to the law, in order to buy property here you must show that it will be your primary residence. But that's hardly ever checked up on within the city;

it's very hard to keep track when, say, married couples split up and start living separately. So-called 'festival flats' that are only used for a couple of nights a year aren't a mass phenomenon, Kurz maintains, less common than in ski resorts in any event, where entire apartment blocks stand empty for most of the time. 'And anyone who's seriously wealthy lives all over the place anyhow,' says the estate agent of his clientele.

The most sought-after locations are districts close to the old city, such as Riedenburg, Nonntal or Morzg, and Aigen and Parsch on the other side of the Salzach. Not the old city itself, however. Living there can be a pain. Old buildings generally have no lift. And then there's the noise, the lack of parking spaces and restricted access to contend with. 'Really stunning, large apartments on the Getreidegasse are unlettable to all practical intents and purposes, even though rents have risen far less steeply over the past decade than house purchase prices,' the estate agent confides. Likewise, offices that don't have easy access are extremely difficult to let.

This has led to a dangerous imbalance in the Old Town, with any number of upmarket shops, chain stores for the most part, as against just a couple of hundred inhabitants and, during the day, thousands of tourists. 'If you walk through the town here at night, the place is deserted, completely deserted. These beautiful squares are bereft of all life, there's absolutely nothing going on there. Nor do you get the feeling this is a student town, in spite of there being thousands of students here, and despite the fact that there are people here clearly making a living,' Markus Hinterhäuser, artistic director of the festival from autumn 2016, complained some years ago.

The Salzburg caricaturist Thomas Wizany has the same axe to grind. In a television interview, he described the city from his perspective as a trained architect:

> If you compare it with Italian cities, then the architecture remains Italian. But the mentality of people here is anything but, in my view. If you walk through this city, it's like you've turned off the soundtrack. These squares weren't even conceived as the city's living spaces where people could meet, either, but rather as showpieces for Catholicism. It's better on the municipal squares like the Alter Markt with the Café Tomaselli, there's a bit more going on there, but then the pavements empty by about eight or nine in the evening. That's really sad.

Perhaps that's one reason why relatively little importance has been attached to the design of alleyways and squares in Salzburg. 'I personally find that really shocking,' says an irritated Alexander Kurz. 'Even in small historic towns in Italy or Croatia, the pavement surfaces are much better, and you could hardly claim that Salzburg has less money to spend.' For decades, this has been an impassioned topic of debate in the city. Politics here, as elsewhere, hasn't yet mastered the art of pleasing all of the people all of the time.

That's particularly in evidence on the Residenzplatz. Unsightly, common-or-garden gravel is the surface that plays host here to Rupertikirtag and the Christmas Market; owing to the ruins of prestigious residential dwellings dating from the Roman city of Juvavum formerly on this site, which lie buried beneath the square, the requirements of historic preservation run counter to the demands of a modern city. Some years ago, trial surfaces laid out using gravel reclaimed from the Salzach were intended to kick-start a modernisation programme. All to no avail. The milled pebbles were deemed not durable enough. At least the tarmac around the edges of the square will now be replaced with classier granite paving slabs, at long last. Even so, there's still plenty of material for debate, given that the area of gravel round the fountain is set to remain.

Another project is already definitively dead. A large bus station on the Kapuzinerberg, designed to better regulate the deluge of visitors, with an entrance on the Vogelweiderstraße and an exit on the Linzergasse. The plans were drawn up and a contractor was even in place, but it never happened. 'The politicians just don't want it,' Alexander Kurz tells me. 'The current old city bus station on the Mönchberg is a godsend, though of course it'd be better if it was bigger.' Nevertheless, at least it was still an existing facility.

And in saying this, Kurz finally arrives at what is evidently Salzburgers' favourite topic – city planning. The 'architecturally unsuccessful objects' on the outskirts, the 'architects' clique' whom politicians do not bring 'enough pressure' to bear on. 'Aside from the new Mozarteum and the university building in the Nonntal, there are very few contemporary public buildings we can feel proud of.'

Yet like everyone else here, he's proud of the city itself. At least, proud of what has been shoehorned in between the Mönchsberg, the Kapuzinerberg and the Festungsberg. The fact that the city beyond the centre is expanding is a boon to the estate agent, less so to the regular citizen. When the sheer volume of people in a city becomes too great, its cosiness disappears. 'We've reached saturation point. As a Salzburger I want to see a halt now in this regard,' says Alexander Kurz. It's a plea for manageability. A vote in favour of smallness.

'Small is beautiful' was the credo of the philosopher Leopold Kohr. And he was a Salzburger.

HUBERT NOWAK, born in 1954, is an Austrian journalist and author. For many years, he covered domestic politics on radio and television and was the presenter of 'Zeit im Bild', the most important TV news programme of the Austrian Broadcasting Corporation (ORF). Later, Nowak was director of the ORF Landesstudio in Salzburg. He is a keen observer of and commentator on the Austrian historical and current cultural and political scene.